Sharing Jesus and Showing Kindness by Dr. Alvin Reid is a must-read for those who want to share their faith but lack confidence in their ability. This book is packed full of practical ideas that pastors, small group leaders, and individual Christians can use to reach their community with the life-changing good news of Jesus Christ. So many books on evangelism are either pep talks or guilt trips on why you should share your faith. Dr. Reid gives you tools to start servant evangelism in your church, Sunday school, small group, or on your own. This is a real-life guide from someone who is practicing everything he writes in this book. I highly endorse *Sharing Jesus and Showing Kindness*!

—Dr. Kevin Bussey, DMin, MDiv, MA,
Professor of Biblical Studies, Highlands College

Alvin has done it again! His latest work, *Sharing Jesus and Showing Kindness* is a manifesto for effectively carrying out the Great Commission via the Great Commandment in an increasingly post-Christian nation. Every pastor, youth minister, small group leader and concerned lay person should read this book and seek to implement this biblical strategy of "serving with our lives" and "sharing with our lips." Well done, faithful Alvin!

—Scott Camp,
evangelist, author, educator,
Ghana Christian University, Accra, Ghana

I have known Dr. Alvin Reid for over thirty years. In that time we have done a lot of servant evangelism ministry together in various different settings. I know Alvin's heart for the unsaved! So please believe me when I say that *Sharing Jesus and Showing Kindness* is a must read for every Christian! In a culture that often sees the church as uncaring and callous, Alvin gives numerous practical approaches and ideas to break that mold in order to engage in authentic gospel conversations! That said, I endorse *Sharing Jesus and Showing Kindness* with no reservations!

—Dr. David Wheeler,
Professor of Evangelism,
Sr. Executive Director LU Shepherd, Liberty University

Wow! My friend Alvin Reid's book *Sharing Jesus and Showing Kindness* is fire! My favorite line is: "Churches will be revitalized when the gospel becomes prioritized." Alvin is not only a gifted writer, but he lives and breathes what these pages are about. This book is biblical, motivational, practical, and highly instructional. It's an excellent resource to help you be intentional about showing kindness and sharing Jesus with others. I encourage every pastor, deacon, and church leader to get it, read it, and pass it on to others.

—Dr. Bill Wilks,
Pastor, NorthPark Baptist Church, Trussville,
Alabama; author and trainer, D-Life

Sharing
Jesus

Showing
Kindness

Mobilizing Disciple-Makers
Through Servant Evangelism

ALVIN REID

IRON
STREAM

Birmingham, Alabama

Sharing Jesus and Showing Kindness

Iron Stream Media
100 Missionary Ridge
Birmingham, AL 35242
IronStreamMedia.com

Library of Congress Control Number: 2023946435

Cover design by Jonathan Lewis / Jonlin Creative

ISBN: 978-1-56309-690-7 (paperback)
ISBN: 978-1-56309-692-1 (ebook)

1 2 3 4 5—28 27 26 25 24

To David Wheeler, my longtime friend and encourager. You are a legend in the practice of servant evangelism, and I thank you for your influence on my life. To Steve Sjogren, the entrepreneurial pastor who pioneered and promoted servant evangelism. Thanks for your continued encouragement in evangelism.

To John Herring, my friend, brother, and CEO at Iron Stream Media. Thanks for believing in me. Kevin Bussey, professor at Highlands College and longtime friend, you are a constant source of encouragement. Jeff Gardner, I owe you so much. How I love you and your family! Scott Camp, you chased me down and built me up. Every man needs a brother like you. To Bill Wilks, for your devotion to disciple-making. And to Church of the Highlands, which shares Jesus and shows kindness by serving others better than any church I know!

To Pam, my constant encourager, friend, and love. You have changed my life. To our children and grandchildren: you bring us such joy.

To all those friends, too many to name, who have walked with me, sharing good news and showing kindness along the way.

To every pastor, leader, and Christian who desires to make an impact for Christ in this changing world through the gospel.

To every follower of Jesus who chooses compassion over cynicism, truth and grace over power and control, humility over hubris, and kindness over cruelty, may we see a disciple-making movement that stands firm on the gospel and shows the kindness of God's love.

Contents

Introduction

Just the other day a man came up to me after a worship service. He knew I had a background in evangelism and asked if I had time for a question.

"Of course," I said.

Looking across at the large auditorium and the people milling around, he asked, "How are we going to get Christians like these who gather in churches week after week to get over the shock of how the world has changed and get back to telling the world about Jesus?"

In his question, he identified an apparent contradiction between how Christianity is exhibited in gathered worship services compared to everyday life. It reminds me of what Steven Pressfield says in *The War of Art*: "Most of us have two lives. The life we live, and the unlived life within us."[1] He said that to aspiring writers, but it also describes the American church. On the one hand, there is the life evident in churches across America weekly as the faithful sing passionately, greet one another warmly, and serve faithfully. But there is an unlived life experienced by so many church members. These same believers—or a host of them—seem far more inclined to sing about Jesus weekly than to talk about Him daily.

I don't say that to be critical but to acknowledge what the man's question revealed. He didn't have to explain what he meant. I see it all the time. It comes up in my small group. I feel it, too. You don't have to be a philosopher of culture or a theologian to understand that our world has shifted radically in a short time. Author and *New York Times* writer Ross Douthat observed a similar contradiction: while the pandemic halted the world for a bit in 2020—jolting us all in different ways—it created an acceleration of change at the time. It's like the world shut down in March 2020 and we suddenly woke up in 2030.[2] The pace of life accelerated, strife and distrust elevated, and evil escalated faster than we could've imagined. I've heard a number of pastors say something like, "Seminary never prepared me for what we're dealing with today!"

What's the church to do?

Retreat in fear, turning our church buildings and homes into bomb shelters, shielded from a broken world?

Respond in anger, preaching our disgust at people like an angry neighbor yelling at people to get off his yard?

Walk on eggshells, timidly trying to "love" people without speaking the truth?

No, these won't do. In times like this, we cut through the activities that fill our calendars, disconnect from social media, and look instead to the Lord above.

We return to our core as followers of Jesus.

Love God.

Love people.

Make disciples.

This threefold description of the mission of the church gets a lot of play these days. I'm glad to see it. There is a growing realization that the church of the Lord Jesus Christ needs to get back to making the main thing the main thing, not only because the world seems to be losing its grip but also to encourage frustrated and anxious believers.

The **Great Commandment** calls us to love God above all and our neighbor as we love ourselves. "Jesus replied, 'You shall love the

Lord your God with all your heart and with all your soul and with all your mind.' And the second is like it: 'You shall love your neighbor as yourself'" (Matthew 22:37–38).

You can't love people and loathe them simultaneously.

You can't reach people and hate them at the same time.

The **Great Commission** compels us to go into the world to make disciples who make disciples. Jesus said, "All authority in heaven and on earth has been given to me. Go therefore and make disciples of all the nations, baptizing them in the name of the Father and of the Son and of the Holy Spirit, teaching them to observe everything that I have commanded you. And look, I am with you always, to the end of the age" (Matthew 28:18–20).

You can't obey this commission and be separated from the people we are called to reach.

These words of our Lord get to the core of our mission. But how do we live this today?

I'm a teacher. A teacher is a person who helps other people *get* it, whatever *it* may be. For me, more than anything, *it* involves helping people who love Jesus do what God has put in their hearts but find hard to do: telling others the good news found in Jesus Christ. Nothing lights my fire or cranks my engine like seeing a brother or sister in Christ who gets freaked out at the thought of telling someone about Jesus discover they can do it, and then they do!

Yes, we must be willing to step outside our comfort zones to grow in any area of our life. Sure, there is a learning curve where we can get better over time. There are skills we can learn to help us. I'm going to show you just how to help those you lead recapture a passion for reaching people—whether you are a pastor leading a church, a staff member overseeing a ministry, a small group leader shepherding a group, a youth pastor leading a group of students, parents leading their children, or any believer seeking to grow—all these and more.

In this book, you are going to see a simple approach that a family can do together in their neighborhood, a youth group can do on a weekend, or a whole church can do in a variety of ways throughout the year. It requires little training, no profound people skills, or theological brilliance. It's a practical way to bring together the lives we currently live and the unlived life within.

I'm talking about seeing those who need Jesus with eyes of compassion, then personally or with fellow believers finding ways to show kindness in a world where kindness is in short supply. And as we do, to tell people good news—the best news—of life in Jesus's name.

I want to tell you what this looks like and show you how you can implement it in your church to mobilize believers to impact your community, creating a revitalized church. I've seen this happen again and again. God can take broken people who love Him and others and do remarkable things.

Let's get started.

1

Momentum

Moving from Stuck to Stirred

Be kind and compassionate to one another, forgiving each other, just as in Christ God forgave you.

—Ephesians 4:32 NIV

We can, with wisdom, humility, kindness, and the Holy Spirit's empowerment, maybe remove some of the debris that prevents people from seeing Jesus clearly.

—Andy Bannister

Imagine a beautiful April Sunday in Charlotte, North Carolina. The sky seems like a canvas painted Tar Heel blue. The air is crisp and cool but warming up—the perfect day to be outside. We're at the First Baptist Church in downtown Charlotte where everyone from youth through senior adults gather together in the auditorium during the Sunday school hour. I spend that hour teaching some of what you're going to be reading here about sharing Jesus and showing kindness. In the worship service, I preach from John 4 where Jesus showed kindness to the woman at the well. She believed and became a missionary on the spot. "If God can use an outcast woman,

He can use you!" I proclaim, adding, "All because Jesus spoke to her with kindness at a well."

That afternoon following lunch together, hundreds of people spread across the city in groups to show and share Jesus through projects prepared by leaders. I join a group sharing Christ by washing cars for free. The church advertised the day as "First Loves Charlotte." It was so successful that the *Charlotte Observer* ran a full-page spread with the theme as the headline.

Later in the afternoon, we gather to share experiences with one another. People are stoked—is this a group doing *evangelism* or a crowd at a Carolina Panthers game? Laughter, smiles, and applause mark the time as we hear accounts of church members serving, some sharing Christ for the first time, and stories of salvation.

That day years ago was so powerful that we did it again the next spring. I've seen this happen again and again, like on Saturday afternoons at youth Disciple Now events after hours of showing and sharing Jesus or following a car wash with ministry students where two students led someone to Christ for the first time ever. These stories never get old. Nothing builds enthusiasm and creates momentum for the things nearest to God's heart than sharing the gospel and serving people. But it seems the times of celebrating the gospel and its impact are not as evident as in the past.

Reality Check

Now imagine going to the doctor because you know something is wrong, but you aren't prepared to hear just how bad things are. Ever been there? For several years, I've had an issue with walking far or standing for long periods mainly from an artificial hip I've had for over twenty-five years. I worked around this by speaking from a stool and avoiding activities requiring long walks. But in December

2022, I began experiencing severe nerve pain in my pelvic area. OK, severe is too mild of a word. It was horrible! An MRI and a visit to a neurosurgeon showed me what I didn't want to admit: my L2, L3, and L4 vertebrae were trashed. I had the reality check I could no longer ignore. I'm grateful to report that my surgeon performed robotic spinal fusion surgery in March of 2023, and today as I type this, I was able to walk one mile nonstop for the first time in years! I feel better than I have in a long time, only because I got real about the brokenness in my spine.

It's time for the American church to get real about the Great Commission. Evangelism is not the passion, priority, or practice of most Christians or churches in America today. That's not just my opinion; I've spoken to leaders from major organizations, pastors, and evangelists who echo this evaluation. Sharing Jesus is not even a consistent practice of a lot of pastors and church leaders. I don't say this to be critical or shaming. My doctor didn't shame me when he reviewed my MRI. He also didn't deny what would happen if I didn't take drastic measures.

I'm an encourager by nature, and that's the aim of this book: to encourage you, equip you, and help you engage others for Jesus. But the passion we read about in Acts of believers who could not stop showing kindness to others and speaking about Jesus is not as evident today.

Recent studies consistently highlight this. In the fall of 2022, the Great Commission Research Network asked pastors to name the greatest challenges they foresaw for 2023. Out of fifty categories, what do you think were the top two in the survey? They were:

1. Mobilizing believers for evangelism.
2. A concern for evangelism.[1]

These top challenges weren't the top two from fifty possible evangelism issues but were the only two evangelism choices out of fifty from myriad topics including "leadership training" (ranked seventeenth), "Christian nationalism" (twenty-ninth), "church conflict" (thirty-fifth), and "technology" (thirty-eighth). There was one topic related to but not specifically naming evangelism ranked thirty-sixth, "making the gospel attractive." Out of the important issues from gender identity to racism and from false doctrine to poverty, pastors put the two specific topics related to evangelism at the top.

> The top two challenges facing the church according to pastors: mobilizing believers for evangelism and a concern for evangelism.
>
> —Great Commission Research Network

Compare that to a Lifeway Research survey of one thousand pastors released in 2022. The largest percentage of pastors identified two issues equally that must be addressed: stress (the pandemic accelerated this) and disciple making (each with 63 percent).[2]

Another study just released is documented in *The Great Dechurching* by Jim Davis and Michael S. Graham, with research from Ryan Burge. Their research found that "we are in the middle of the largest and fastest religious shift in the history of our country."[3] About forty million adults, or 16 percent of the population, no longer attend church. These are the dechurched. These are the ***dones***; they were involved in church but are done with it, at least for now. The shift began accelerating in the 1990s. While the Assemblies of God and nondenominational churches continue to grow, major denominations including Baptists, Methodists, and others are in decline.

We live in a day where growth is often seen more in the **nones** and the **dones** than the church. The **nones** refer to those who identify their religious commitment as unaffiliated or "none." Their numbers have risen significantly in recent decades as it's become socially acceptable to be unaffiliated. The acceleration is seen especially—and for the church, ominously—in younger generations.

- *Nones* grew from 16 percent to 29 percent of the population from 2007–2021.[4]

- Thirty-one percent of adults aged 30–39 raised in a Christian context now identify as *nones*; 73 percent of adults 30–39 raised religiously unaffiliated identify as *nones*. In other words, being unaffiliated is "stickier" with young adults than being Christian.[5]

- Over one-third (34 percent) of Gen Z are *nones*, an increase from 29 percent among millennials, 25 percent of Gen X, and 18 percent of baby boomers.[6]

- Almost one in five (18 percent) of Gen Z are agnostic or atheist, double from the baby boomer generation (about one in ten, or 9 percent).[7]

In 2021, church membership in the US fell below 50 percent for the first time in the eighty years Gallup has tracked the numbers.[8] Those who identify as Christian also declined from 78 percent to 63 percent of the US population.[9]

> To reach the dechurched *dones* and the unaffiliated *nones*, we need a church awakened to the gospel's power and engaged with unchurched people.

OK, that's the bad news, which is why we need the good news. The reality is that we've lost the home field advantage in America today. But the gospel travels well, as we see in Acts with the first century church and in many places where the gospel is growing like China and sub-Saharan Africa today. The gospel has not lost its power, we've just lost our focus.

The current diagnosis is not good. But the gospel is still the power of God, and there are millions who love Jesus and want to make an impact for God's glory.

A physical therapist told me the main reason people get hurt is because they stop moving. Sitting all day and becoming a couch potato at night is a recipe for health problems. And then they get injured. Inactivity is not only bad for your physical health; it's bad for your spiritual health. Too many Christians are stuck, inactive and hesitant in their witness. It's easy to be uncertain and over-whelmed today. But if Jesus changed your life and the Spirit of God dwells within you, a passion for glorifying God and helping others is deep within you. You were reconciled to show the world our great God's kindness through Christ and to tell the world what Jesus has done for us (2 Corinthians 5:15–21)!

Time to Change

It's time for a change. How did we lose the idea that the gospel is good news for a broken world, that Jesus gave the Great Commission—not the Great Suggestion—to every believer, and that we have no greater hope for a broken world? More importantly, how do we recover?

The past few years we've been socially distanced, divided, and depressed, with mental health numbers at historic levels. The church has not been immune to the challenges of our time. The answer for the church is the answer the world needs: the power of the gospel.

When you read the book of Acts, you see the dominant person in the growth and spread of the gospel is not a person—at least not like you and me. The Holy Spirit is the main Person in the story, as Jesus had said He would be (John 14:15–17). If we want to see a stirring movement of gospel impact by showing and sharing Jesus, we will need the unparalleled power of the Spirit. He is the one calling the church to action and filling them with power; He will do the same today!

Features of the work of the Spirit in Acts:

1. Four times the Spirit speaks in a direct quote, and in every case, He said "Go." See Acts 8:29–35; 10:19–20; 13:2 (where He set apart Saul and Barnabas for formal missionary work); and 28:25–26.

2. Consistently, when the Spirit filled believers, their immediate response was to share Christ: Acts 2:4, 11; 4:8, 31; 6:3, 7; 9:17, 20; 11:24; 13:9.[10]

Recovering Gospel Traction Through Servant Evangelism

What if I told you there is a way to equip your church to share Christ in a way that is both effective and encouraging? It's true.

There is a way to bring nervous Christians out of their shells to discover confidence and compassion for the broken people in your community.

I've seen it again and again: nervous Christians becoming bold witnesses when they learned to share Jesus not as professional communicators but just by showing Jesus and then sharing good news:

- I've seen a timid layman become a radical soul winner after a couple of days of paying for people's laundry in South Carolina, where he led several to Jesus himself.
- I've seen it at a free car wash where a young minister led a total stranger for the first time and wept with joy.
- I've seen it in teenagers going door-to-door giving packs of light bulbs to people, telling them about Jesus, the Light of the World.

I'm talking about **servant evangelism**. It's a concept I first heard about from Steve Sjogren, a pastor in Ohio at the time we met, and from my dear friend David Wheeler, who has put this into practice for years with students at Liberty University.

What is it about servant evangelism that causes such joy and enthusiasm? The key is understanding what it is.

Servant evangelism: when believers intentionally show the good news through our lives in order to share the good news with our lips.

It's that simple and, yet, that profound. You see, every person who knows Jesus, who has been forgiven and raised to new life in Christ, and who has the Holy Spirit within has a desire to bring glory to God and do good for others. It's built into our born-again

DNA. But in our hyper-driven, complex world where in an average day we make about thirty-five thousand decisions, we are often distracted to the point that we can't hear the Spirit's voice in our efforts to make it through another busy day. When we tap into the spiritual DNA God put into us—like joining with other believers to focus on sharing the good news with their community—we quickly respond with enthusiasm because we know we are doing something that matters in eternity, which is far more important than deciding what to eat for lunch.

Servant evangelism is so simple that it is easily missed: get a group of believers, like your family, a class, small group, or a few folks from your church and begin practicing simple acts of kindness with an *intentional* aim toward evangelism. In many cases, such acts of kindness open the door for the greatest act of kindness a Christian can give: the gospel.

We show good news through our lives.

Servant evangelism treats others as people rather than projects. We show kindness to people we meet, seeing them as uniquely made in the image of God and someone for whom Jesus died.

If all we do is seek to win someone's soul without caring for them as a person, we fail to live out the Great Commandment even while we are seeking to obey the Great Commission. People are not stupid—they can tell if we care about them. People can tell at least three things by how we treat them:

1. **If we care about them.** *People do not care how much you know about God until they know how much you care for them.* Demonstrating kindness, from praying for a server (with a good tip!) to mowing an unchurched neighbor's lawn, helps people see Christ in us. There is no

compromise of the gospel of Jesus by showing kindness and serving others.

2. **If we believe what we are sharing.** I've observed a bit of a trend in some churches since the pandemic to elevate the importance of serving their communities. This is a good thing, but if we are serving needs without ever speaking about their greatest need for a Savior, what does that say about our belief in the gospel?

3. **If the hand of God is on our lives.** The more we as believers and together as the church demonstrate God's love, the more people will see God at work in us. Let's face it, people who need Jesus aren't impressed by our buildings, worship services, or mission projects. But when they see us showing kindness in our communities, they take notice.

We share good news with our lips.

We serve regardless of how people respond, but our goal is to share the gospel whenever we can. That's what makes it servant *evangelism*. Sometimes churches offer valuable ministries, such as taking a loaf of bread to newcomers, which are helpful, but if they are not explicitly evangelistic, they aren't examples of servant evangelism.

Think about it: how cruel would it be to offer free bottles of water at the park or the ball field, enter a conversation with someone, and then fail to tell them about the Living Water (John 4)? To give a light bulb without telling of the Light of the World (Matthew 5)? To clean a toilet without talking about the only One who can cleanse a person's heart from sin (1 John 1:7)?

We are bombarded daily with needs on our big screens and small screens: the latest crisis in the news, the next hashtag on social media. It never stops unless we (wisely) take time to unplug. There are all sorts of "gospels" being preached to win people to this cause or respond to that crisis. In the whirl of voices, we can forget that the greatest need in the world is for a Savior whose name is Jesus. That's not the only need, but it is the greatest one, so sharing good news verbally matters. We aren't doing random acts of kindness without a greater gospel purpose. When doing an act of kindness, you can say, "I'm just showing the love of Jesus in a practical way," or if asked why you are serving simply say, "Just because we care." Then, as the Holy Spirit opens the door, the witness can share the gospel and/or their testimony of salvation.

We serve in Jesus's name, and we pray the same thing Paul asked of the Colossians:

- That God would open doors to share (Colossians 4:3)
- To proclaim the gospel clearly when we can (4:4)
- To make the most of every opportunity (4:5)
- When we can share Jesus, to do so with words full of grace, seasoned with salt (4:6)
- To be able to answer people as we can (4:6)

You can share Christ verbally without serving others. You can serve others without sharing Christ. But when you combine the two, you have a powerful tool for serving our great God.

Let's be honest; if most of us were given a choice between serving people and sharing Jesus verbally, we are going to pick serving. We tend to drift toward the easiest and least challenging. That's why evangelism and fasting are the two least practiced spiritual disciplines in surveys that some of my doctoral students have done over the years.

We also must look honestly at history. Over the past century when groups have emphasized both the demonstration and the proclamation of the gospel, inevitably proclamation gets lost in serving. But it doesn't have to be that way. It wasn't that way in the early church. You can serve and share, proclaim Christ's love and picture it with good deeds, and do gracious deeds while sharing the truth of good news.

For Review

Think about those first two challenges mentioned by pastors reported by the Great Commission Network. Answer the following, not to be negative, but to take an honest inventory to move forward.

1. On a scale of 1 to 5, with 5 being high, how effectively is your church being mobilized to share Christ? How can you help?

2. With the same scale, how would you rate your church's concern for evangelism or for reaching people around you? Who are people in your church you might invite to join you when you serve and share Jesus?

3. If you believe your church can do more to reach out into your community for Jesus, rather than being frustrated or defeated by where you are, what small steps might you take to change this?

4. Discuss the statement: You can share Christ verbally without serving others. You can serve others without sharing

Christ. But when you combine the two, you have a power-ful tool for serving our great God.

- Why do we tend to serve more than share?
- How can we help each other share as much as we serve?

You can share Christ verbally without serving others. You can serve others without sharing Christ. But when you combine the two, you have a powerful tool for serving our great God.

2

Passion

*Revitalizing Your Church and
Reaching Your Community*

Love is patient and is kind.

—1 Corinthians 13:4

*Only as we drink down the kindness of the heart of Christ will
we leave in our wake, everywhere we go, the aroma of heaven,
and die one day having startled the world with glimpses of a
divine kindness too great to be boxed in by what we deserve.*

—Dane Ortlund

I like to think of myself as an innovator, or at least an early adopter, someone who loves trying new things. The truth, however, is that I often love the *thought* of new ideas more than putting them into practice. When I first heard about the approach of servant evangelism, I *loved* the idea, but it took some prodding to get me to be all-in as a leader and teacher.

I learned the concept from the best: Steve Sjogren and David Wheeler. Steve planned and built a great church on servant evangelism in Cincinnati. His book *Conspiracy of Kindness* encouraged me greatly. David Wheeler has been a professor for years at Liberty

University. I met up with these men and first learned about servant evangelism at a conference David hosted in Indianapolis when he was evangelism director for the State Convention of Baptists in Indiana. He had invited Steve and me both to speak there, and I found the concept of servant evangelism intriguing.

Have you ever gone to a conference or to a training event and learned some things you just knew would be awesome, but when push came to shove, you just didn't quite have the initiative required to make it happen when you got back home? It's just easier to stick with the status quo, isn't it? Maybe I'm the only person like that, but I doubt it. That's why the Holy Spirit's presence in our lives is so important. The conference with Steve and David in Indiana was in early February, just after the spring semester began for my evangelism classes. I went through the entire spring semester with good intentions about implementing servant evangelism in my evangelism classes. But it didn't happen.

That status quo is a *beast*.

Here's how awesome the Holy Spirit is. Though I missed the spring window, I got another chance. I was scheduled to teach a personal evangelism class that met Monday through Friday for two weeks at the start of the summer. I had already planned to have class in the morning and go out to witness—basically going door-to-door—four days for each of the two weeks all afternoon. I expected fifteen to twenty students, so organizing groups to go out in twos and threes was not too challenging. When I saw that sixty had signed up, I didn't know whether to spit or wind my watch! Getting that many students organized to go out every afternoon was a bit overwhelming. It was out of desperation that I decided it would be a good time to try servant evangelism with my students. Necessity is the mother of invention, right?

Remember Steve Sjogren I mentioned above? When we met at that conference, he was the founding and current pastor of Vineyard Church in Cincinnati, Ohio. I told the class they were going to be the guinea pigs as we were going to put servant evangelism into action.

I told them how Steve's church had exploded with growth through servant evangelism. Guess what happened when I mentioned this in class? I had a student *in that very class* who had come from Steve's church! At a Baptist seminary, no less. This fellow was the only student from a Vineyard church I had ever seen at our school. He told us more about servant evangelism and helped a lot to organize students.

So, the Holy Spirit pushed me to try something new *and* provided someone to help, but He did more. In those afternoons as we went out to show and share Christ, we saw over two dozen people saved, including some remarkable examples.

In a two-week long personal evangelism class, the Holy Spirit did amazing things through sharing Jesus and showing kindness:

- A former Hindu trusted Jesus at a car wash where the student witnessing was a former Hindu!

- A man driving through town one afternoon said he'd just said out loud, "Why doesn't anyone do anything to help people anymore?" He turned the corner and drove right into a free car wash we were doing. I talked to him but then turned to a student to witness; that student led him to Jesus. It was the first time he'd ever led someone to Christ!

We had stories like that every day. Though it's not a large sample size, I discovered that in those two weeks people were more than twice as likely to listen to someone share Christ when in the context of being served than they would be in other settings. And a higher percentage responded to the gospel in salvation. The first two weeks I put this into practice I became a believer!

Recovering a New Testament Approach

Helpless. Ever felt that way?

Over forty years old, this nameless man appears early in Acts 3. All his life he'd been lame. He couldn't even go to beg without the help of others. At least he had others to carry him by the temple gate to ask for aid. But today, all he could think about was the oppressive heat of the sun bearing down on him. No shade. No relief. It was about three in the afternoon.

As the lame man lay by the temple gate, Peter and John met him. They stopped. They had time for a helpless man who begged them for a handout. Peter said to him, "I do not have silver or gold, but what I have I will give you. In the name of Jesus Christ of Nazareth, get up and walk!" (Acts 3:6). The man got up and began walking and leaping and praising God! I would do the same if I were in his condition. Peter and John showed the man an "act of kindness" (Acts 4:9 NIV), which led to over five thousand coming to Christ (4:4).

Outcast. Ever known people like that?

Sure, Zach had wealth and a lot of it. But what good is wealth if you have no one to share it with? He had a lot of something heavier than all his coins—the weight of guilt. He could buy anything materially he wanted, but he couldn't buy acceptance. He was a publican, a tax collector; in fact, he was chief among his profession. Ridiculed for his short stature and criticized for his occupation, Zach needed someone to care.

You know Zach, or Zaccheus, the "wee little man" from vacation Bible school. Jesus showed him kindness, joining this outcast for dinner. People complained that Jesus was going to be the guest of such a sinner. But Jesus said, "Today salvation has come to this house" (Luke 19:9). The man was changed. Jesus showed kindness and shared good news.

Broken. Ever found yourself in this place?

The woman came to the well to get water, and yet, this daily routine served as one more reminder of her broken life. She couldn't go to the well when other women did; she had to come alone. As the noontime sun bore down on her weary body, she walked in solitude, reflecting on the pain of one broken relationship after another. She longed to worship God, but would God care for a broken woman of Samaria? If only someone could show her the way.

When she got to the well, Jesus was there, weary as well from His journey. He spoke words of kindness to her. He treated her differently than others. She welcomed His message and suddenly went from broken mistress to bold missionary, inviting others to hear Him. And many believed in Jesus (John 4:39–41). Kindness shown, good news shared.

Again and again in the life of Jesus and the early church, we see a demonstration of kindness and the proclamation of the gospel. Here are just a few examples from Acts:

- Widows were being neglected. When the church set people apart to serve them, more people came to Christ (Acts 6:7).

- Philip, led by an angel to the desert, encountered the Ethiopian eunuch. Philip showed kindness by asking the man if he understood what he read (Acts 8:30–35). Philip helped him to understand, shared the gospel, and the man believed (verses 36–39).

- Peter healed Aeneas and raised Tabitha to life. In each of these miraculous acts of kindness, people turned to the Lord as a result (Acts 9:35, 42).

Evangelism literally means telling good news, good news we can show with our lives and speak with our lips. I think we can all agree that we live in a day badly in need of good news.

This approach doesn't deny the importance of standing for truth and defending the faith. But it does recognize that many people will be reached not with an intellectual argument but by a demonstration of compassion. Start with the heart and move to the head through the work of your hands.

When you study the Gospels, you see Jesus responded to three different groups of people in three distinct ways. *First, when Jesus encountered broken people, He showed great compassion.* Think about the woman of Samaria, the many accounts of people He healed, and how He dined with sinners and was criticized for doing so. *Second, He confronted the religious hypocrites (the people who criticized His compassion).* Just read Matthew 23 to see how He excoriated this crowd. *Finally, He expected total surrender from those who followed him (Luke 9:23, for instance).* In my experience, we've treated the lost world too often like Jesus treated the religious leaders. We will encounter self-righteous people who need to be challenged, but I meet far more people today who don't know Jesus who are broken, searching, and hurt.

Effective Witness in a Changing Culture

For a few decades we saw the rise of entrepreneurial megachurches who reached vast numbers of baby boomers with an attractional focus. Many of these churches were planted by gifted leaders like Rick Warren, Andy Stanley, and Craig Groeschel, with thousands of churches embracing the model. These churches were effective at reaching people by simply encouraging their congregations to invest in people and invite them to services to hear the gospel. That's still effective for many, but with church attendance shrinking and the nones and dones growing, churches must return to the "go and tell" approach seen in Acts rather than a purely "come and see" strategy. Servant evangelism offers a way for the church to go and tell *and* go and show God's love.

I mentioned the book *The Great Dechurching* by Davis and Graham and its description of the largest shift in American history. They give ominous information about younger generations: "In 2016 about 39 percent of Generation Z were nones. . . . Today that is up to 44.4 percent."[1] With Gen Alpha now emerging, we are trending toward *half* of younger generations being religiously unaffiliated. How do we reclaim the dechurched and reach the unchurched? Davis and Graham nail it: they "need to see a gospel that isn't just true but is also good and beautiful. They will likely need to see the gospel *tangibly demonstrated* before they have much interest in it being proclaimed."[2] I have seen this confirmed again and again through servant evangelism efforts where some of the most unchurched people—and those fed up with church—found our work and message to be compelling and interesting.

Our changing culture and its polarization mean we meet more people than ever who aren't impressed or interested when we start our witness with "Thus says the Lord" and tell them what the Bible says. We love the Bible and know its life-changing message. But they aren't so sure. Like Jesus, we want to start where people are and connect so they will more likely hear what we have to say. When we begin gospel opportunities with serving, it opens the door for sharing. Servant evangelism gives a simple pathway to show and share the good news.

Showing kindness and sharing Jesus not only helps to engage with people who don't know Christ; it helps believers in their growth as well. The more a Christian sees people with compassion and a servant's heart, they will want to become more like Jesus. The more we connect with people by showing kindness, the easier it becomes to speak of our Savior.

Here's a vital point I will make repeatedly. You'll read many examples of servant evangelism in these pages. But don't miss this huge fact: these projects are *practice* to help believers move more toward a mindset of servanthood and a Great Commission focus daily.

> The servant evangelism projects you participate in are important, but they are intended for something more important. They are practice to help you become a more serving and sharing Christian in your everyday world.

The goal is not to get a good response to a project once. It's to get people regularly engaged in serving Jesus together while sharing the good news. The ultimate goal is to have a church full of believers who consistently think about their neighbors, coworkers, and friends who need Jesus so they can be led by the Holy Spirit to serve and share Christ with those they care most about.

That's how a movement is born. In our rapidly changing world, it's natural to shift to a mindset of maintaining our institutions through the shifts rather than on advancing a movement. The New Testament church focused on advancing a gospel movement, not establishing and maintaining institutions. Note the difference:

Church Focused on Maintaining	Church as a Movement
Christianity is mainly a **place**: "I go to church on Sunday."	Christianity is mainly a **people** on a mission: "I am the church 24-7."

Christianity is **mainly** a set of doctrines to believe intellectually.	Christianity is both doctrines to be believed **and** a life to be lived.
Christianity is best seen by the activity **within** the church facility.	Christianity is best seen by its impact **outside** the church building in the culture.
The local church is a **hotel** for saints to be fed, wed, and buried when dead.	The local church is a **hospital** for sinners to find healing and life.[3]

The Pivot Servant Evangelism Provides

At another time when our country faced a dramatic and difficult shift, President Franklin D. Roosevelt delivered one of the most iconic speeches in American history. The year was 1933, and the Great Depression ravaged the nation. In his inaugural address, FDR made the famous statement: "Let me assert my firm belief that the only thing we have to fear is fear itself—nameless, unreasoning, unjustified terror which paralyzes needed efforts to convert retreat into advance."[4] We remember "the only thing we have to fear is fear itself" part. But look again at the end of the sentence where he calls the nation to pivot, to "convert retreat into advance." That's the pivot the church needs. This is not the time to retreat. It's the time to get out of our chairs and into the community. It's time to stop sweating the moral rot around us and start showing kindness while sharing Jesus. It's time to move from the path of least resistance to the path of greatest obedience.

> It's time to move from the path of least resistance to the path of greatest obedience.

But the way to do this is not by marshalling the congregation like Navy SEALs about to go into combat but by guiding them as a good shepherd. We don't need more type A's yelling at people. (I say that as a type A!) We need more encouragers like Barnabas at Antioch (Acts 11:22–24).

I will unpack this more in chapter 5 when I talk about implementation, but here's a glimpse of how I do it. My aim is to bring people together rather than alienate them. I'm not going to scold people who don't witness but will show them how God saved them for this.

When I train believers at a church or youth group in servant evangelism, I repeat this often: if the thought of telling someone about Jesus terrifies you, it's OK. Come and join us, and I promise you that you won't have to say a word if you don't want to. Just serve and watch and learn! At one church, a senior adult lady confessed to me that she had been a Christian for fifty-plus years but had never once shared Jesus until she nervously joined our group at a car wash. The only reason she did so was because I promised she didn't have to say a word. Guess what happened? Over the time of the car wash, she moved from sitting and watching to helping out some to talking to people. No one made her, but her confidence soared as she witnessed people witnessing.

Christian, You Were Made for This!

Every single person who has met Jesus and has the Holy Spirit shares this in common: we all want to honor and obey our Lord and be led by the Spirit. We know we can't do that and ignore the Great Commission or the Spirit's promptings when we think of the lost around us. You were made for this! But for several reasons actually speaking up for Jesus is hard, including these:

- We don't see evangelism modeled regularly, and many believers have never seen another Christian share Christ personally.

- We don't see evangelism modeled as a priority in our churches or our discipleship, so we fill the burden for reaching people with other things—good things, like a passion for worshiping together, for fellowship, or others.

- We feel so inadequate or ill-equipped that we think others should do it instead of us.

Whatever the reason, far too many believers are missing out! When my daughter Hannah was learning to swim, she loved the pool but was terrified to swim underwater. When she realized there was so much more pool to enjoy underneath the surface, she became almost amphibious! Too many Christians live in the kiddie pool when God wants us to dive deep by faith. Servant evangelism helps us to do that in ways that encourage rather than discourage. I've seen this over and over again, especially in teenagers. This makes me think that a great way to reach the unchurched and dechurched in younger generations is the same way to keep them engaged in church: servant evangelism. I've seen young people move from terrified to tenacious in their witness this way.

Young people just like Miranda.

I was speaking at a youth Disciple Now (DNow) weekend years ago in the tidewater area of Virginia. Some teens did a car wash and other projects. The church was in a community where simply going door-to-door worked well, so we organized the youth group into groups to canvass an area while offering four-packs of light bulbs as we went. We planned to have two teams of three each walk down both sides of the street. I asked the most terrified teens to come with me because I liked to do the talking. Two high school sophomores raised their hands: Ashley and Miranda. You could see the fear in their eyes! I told them not to worry. One of them could carry the bulbs to hand out while the other wrote down any information we gathered. I would talk.

As we went to the first door, I said, "Boo!" and the ladies jumped. They soon learned that if you are friendly, most people you meet are friendly too. We met some nice people, talked briefly with some, and kept moving. Then I knocked on a door where an older dude jerked the door open suddenly and yelled, "What do you want?"

This guy was big, like fill-the-entire-doorway big. He wore a flannel shirt and had a scowl on his face. He acted like we interrupted something important like watching NASCAR and having a cold one. He was intimidating.

I could feel Ashley and Miranda shaking in fear behind me. But I was no novice, so I continued, "Hi, sir, I'm Alvin. This is Ashley and Miranda, and we are your neighbors from the . . ." I didn't finish the sentence. As soon as he heard the church name, he kicked open the screen door and yelled in my face angrily, "I can't stand that church!"

Makes you want to go out knocking on doors, doesn't it?

What would you do? Here's what I did: I just reacted. The moment he got up in my grill, I punched him right in the face as hard as I could. I had to defend those young ladies, right?

OK, I didn't do that. He scared me! Doing that would be *evandalism*, not evangelism. But I saw something in his expression that made me wonder if he was really a threat. I took a chance and, not exactly sure why, said, "Sir, I'm wondering if you are a member of the church and are just having fun with us."

He stopped, tilted his head, and laughed. "How did you know that?" he asked. I told him I had no idea, but I've done this a lot and had a hunch. It was a fairly large church; the girls didn't recognize him.

He and I laughed about the whole scenario. But Ashley and Miranda missed that last part. They thought the dude was going to mess us up! We all (finally) had a great laugh.

You might think that day would cause those ladies to never talk about Jesus. But Miranda and I kept in touch for years, even until she was a college student. In fact, I told this story with her permission when I spoke as a guest in her evangelism class at Liberty University. That day giving out light bulbs represented a big part of her faith development.

There are so many Mirandas in our churches. They want to serve Jesus. They care about a lost world. But they need encouragement. They need practice. They need to be pushed. Sharing and showing Jesus can be just the push they need.

For Review

1. What are next steps you can take to show kindness and share Jesus with others?

2. The point was made that any outreach projects should be seen not as an end to themselves but as practice to help us develop more of a lifestyle of serving and sharing. Why do we tend to do the minimum—like completing a project—rather than incorporating experiences as a part of our ongoing growth?

> Young adults "need to see a gospel that isn't just true but is also good and beautiful. They will likely need to see the gospel tangibly demonstrated before they have much interest in it being proclaimed."
>
> —Davis and Graham, *The Great Dechurching*

3

Mobilization

Energizing Believers to Show and
Share Jesus

> *If we are being called to account today for an act of kind-*
> *ness shown to a man who was lame and are being asked*
> *how he was healed, then know this, you and all the people*
> *of Israel: It is by the name of Jesus Christ of Nazareth,*
> *whom you crucified but whom God raised from the dead,*
> *that this man stands before you healed.*
>
> —Acts 4:9–10 NIV

> *Being civil and decent and kind is the bedrock of career*
> *success, as well as personal fulfillment.*
>
> —Tom Peters, *In Search of Excellence*

For too long now, too many believers have felt intimidated, inadequate, or incapable when it comes to sharing Jesus. We live in a win/lose, all-or-nothing world where it may seem that if we don't win someone to Christ when we witness, we must be failures. But if that were the case, Jesus would be a failure too! No, success is in the sharing. Joy comes when we simply obey.

When the only stories the church hears about witnessing are dramatic tales of amazing conversions, evangelism may seem beyond most believers. But the reality is we spend a lot more time in evangelism sowing gospel seeds than reaping. We sow the seed, and God does the harvesting.

Some feel inadequate because they think they have been disqualified from a past failure. Here's the good news about the good news: God only uses broken people because we are all He has!

There are so many reasons servant evangelism gives your church a powerful way to show and share Christ, but here are seven reasons it works so well today.

> God only uses broken people because we are all He has!

1. Sharing Jesus Through Showing Kindness Is Biblical: We Often See the Gospel Displayed Through Serving and Hear It Declared Through Speaking.

The primary reason we should practice servant evangelism is not because it works—though it does—but because it is consistent with Scripture. We read in Matthew 9:35 how Jesus taught in the synagogues, preached the gospel, and healed people. That's a powerful summary of showing and sharing good news! In Luke 10, just after sending out a large group to share the good news, a man asked Him about eternal life. In that context, they discussed the Great Commandment, and then Jesus told the story of the Good Samaritan. Showing kindness wasn't mutually exclusive from sharing the good news of eternal life for our Lord.

Jesus often showed compassion for the hurting while telling the message of salvation. He delivered a demon-possessed man in Mark 5, healed a blind man in John 9, and showed mercy to the woman caught in adultery in John 8, to name a few. Serving others was a hallmark of Jesus's earthly ministry. The simple act of Jesus washing the disciples' feet in John 13 is one of the more defining expressions of His earthly ministry.

We see this continue in the early church in Acts. I've already mentioned Peter and John in Acts 3 when the lame beggar was healed and began to praise God. Or think about Paul and Silas in the Philippian jail in Acts 16. When they were miraculously released, they didn't flee but thought of the welfare of the jailer. What happened? The jailer and his family came to Jesus.

2. Sharing Jesus While Showing Kindness Is Effective at Reaching People in Today's Culture.

We don't want to be driven by pragmatism, but neither do we want to hold on to methods just because they worked years ago. Whether we want to admit it or not, we live in a post-Christian culture. Believers are in the minority today. Societal views about marriage, sexuality, and many other issues no longer parallel our biblical convictions. But remember that the first Christians lived in a pagan Roman culture where they were only a tiny fraction of the population for a long time. And yet, the gospel flourished and spread as passionate believers put the gospel on display and proclaimed it boldly.

The message God gave us for our broken world is the gospel. We are God's Plan A to share this good news, and He hasn't given a Plan B. Servant evangelism offers a way to show a skeptical world how Jesus changes lives, and to share with the world the one true

Story that makes sense of life. It's amazing how simple kindness, like offering a free car wash, opens conversations. When people respond incredulously to an offer to serve them, simply reply, "We're just showing the love of Jesus in a practical way."

People who might otherwise never listen to someone tell the gospel will do so when shown kindness through servant evangelism.

- One former Jehovah's Witness told me how he normally wouldn't let a stranger talk to him about spiritual matters, but as we washed his car, he happily listened to the gospel. He didn't receive Christ, but he heard the good news.

- One young man made it clear he was gay and had rejected everything he had heard as a child growing up in church. As the youth group washed his car, a middle school guy gave his testimony for the first time ever. The young man told us how he'd never seen a group of Christians show him such kindness and how he had only received judgment in the past. I wish I could say he trusted Jesus that day, but he did not. However, he came back after hearing the gospel and asked for more gospel booklets and a Bible. He was visibly moved by our demonstration of the gospel and then by its proclamation.

Too many believers think people are rejecting Jesus when they really reject a modern American caricature of Him. I led a mission trip to New England where we encountered skeptical students, most of whom were impressed when they met our group giving away free sodas and sharing Christ. They continued to come back to talk, moved that the group came all the way from North Carolina to do this. During the next three days as we showed up, shared love, and spoke about Christ, six formerly unchurched young adults eventually gave their lives to Christ.

Because the gospel is a message to believe, we can assume the best way to share it is head-to-head, offering truth to convince an unbeliever to understand it and then affirm it by faith. But far more people are reached heart-to-heart than head-to-head, and servant evangelism is powerful here.

> The world gives a thousand different stories to make sense of life, none of which are true. The gospel is the one Story that makes sense of our story!

3. Servant Evangelism Shows Believers the Power of Unity as It Involves Everyone in the Church Community.

When we think about personal evangelism, we may think about that coworker or family member we know who needs Jesus and wonder how we might talk to them personally. That's important, but it's also a lot, especially for a novice at sharing Christ. Servant evangelism moves believers from the hyperindividualism in our world to serving Christ in community. I will unpack just how this happens in chapter 5.

When you think about a Christian and their spiritual growth, where do we usually start? We start with their daily devotional or "quiet" time. That's focused on the individual. But when we read the vast number of "one another" statements in the New Testament, we see the importance of community. We see the early church often described together. And we see that most of the time, people who served the Lord were not alone. In fact, the times they *were* alone (like Jesus with the Samaritan woman in John 4 or Paul in Athens in Acts 17) were exceptional, not the norm. Jesus sent out His disciples as a group. He sent out seventy, again as a group. Paul normally had companions on his missionary journeys. Jesus gave the Great Commission to disciples, not *a* disciple.

You can do servant evangelism alone, but it's most powerful when a group of believers serve together to bring fellowship and encouragement. I've given some examples, but later you will read a list of opportunities to use for large groups of church members in projects such as group car washes, offering sodas at a park, raking leaves, shoveling snow, and so on. The body of Christ can be on mission learning together in the community. Regardless of age, spiritual gift, or expertise, everyone can share in the glorious experience of seeing others come to Christ. Just try taking your small group out once a quarter or once a month to engage in servant evangelism to see how it brings the gospel to life!

Consider this:
In Jeremiah 29, we read how God's people in Babylonian exile are to act as a community. They are told to "build houses and live in them. Plant gardens and eat their produce. . . . Seek the well-being of the city to which I have sent you as exiles. Pray to the LORD for it" (Jeremiah 29:5, 7). As your church seeks the good of your community, gospel-sharing opportunities will arise!

Servant evangelism moves a church from being a *welcoming* community to the next step: being a people marked by *hospitality*. Most churches are fairly welcoming to people who come to their services. But today when less people—especially those who need Jesus—are attending church services, we need to recover the biblical idea of hospitality. It's a far more common concept in the Bible than you may think. Here are just a few examples:

- The part of the Great Commandment where Jesus says to love our neighbors (Matthew 22:39) comes from Leviticus 19:18. Earlier in 19:10, God's people are told to show hospitality to the poor and to strangers/foreigners.

- Jesus showed hospitality to sinners and outcasts by dining with them (Luke 5:29–32; 19:1–10).

- Paul said, "Contribute to the needs of the saints. Pursue hospitality" (Romans 12:13).

4. This Is the Best Entry-Level Evangelism Approach for Believers of All Ages.

You don't have to be thoroughly equipped, have great communication skills, or have an extroverted personality to participate in servant evangelism. Evangelism is caught more than taught, so learning by doing and observing is made possible through this approach. You can have forty Christians organized with only a half dozen who can share Christ confidently, and with those, you can do a number of servant evangelism projects. Just have one of those confident witnesses on each team. Also encourage those who are less confident but who want to share Christ to team up with the seasoned witnesses.

I've spent a lot of years training youth pastors who have heard me say the "evangelism is caught more than taught" mantra. A youth pastor named Glenn told me how he found this to be true. He had a small youth group of less than a dozen and decided to do a car wash. He told the students not to worry, he would do the talking. All they had to do was wash the cars while he sat with the car owner and chatted. During the afternoon, Glenn was able to lead one person to Christ!

Then he told me what resulted from that one afternoon. "Every time we load the youth group in the van, I see something different now," he said. "The last time we went somewhere, we stopped at a gas station, and I couldn't get the students to stop witnessing to the attendant there," he beamed. It's caught more than taught.

Let's face it, evangelism freaks people out. But believers who are terrified to witness can love their neighbors. They can learn to hand out a pack of light bulbs, clean a car windshield, or pay for a load of laundry at a laundromat. This allows the timid to learn from watching others.

My friend David Wheeler and I have often seen God nudge shy people to join a servant evangelism team, watching witnesses in action while they serve. These same shy people soon become witnesses, overcoming their fear. You won't move hesitant witnesses to action by guilt trips or shaming them. But you can by getting them in situations where they see the gospel at work while serving.

You can take a group of people who would not witness to a teddy bear and let them do the physical stuff: repairing a local playground, yard mowing, and more. This is a powerful way to involve families together in the ministry of evangelism. While a five-year-old child may not be able to explain the gospel message fully, they can help hand out sodas at the store or go along with dad and mom as they rake leaves, cook for their neighbors, or feed hurting people at a local mission center. In the end, the family has a great time of fellowship and fun as each individual is reminded about their Great Commission responsibilities. When my kids were younger, we did these often. In fact, my daughter Hannah would scold me if I did a car wash in our area without telling her!

I've spoken in many Christian schools through the years. Some of them have made servant evangelism a part of what they do in their Bible curriculum. Homeschool families can also make this part of their curriculum, involving their children as a family unit or going out as a homeschool network to put their faith into practice.

5. Servant Evangelism Is Fun!

OK, be honest, a lot of Christians equate "fun" and "evangelism" like they equate "healthy" with "eating kale." (I apologize to the three of you who love kale.) Outside of a mission trip to South Africa or other distant lands, I've never seen believers have any more fun doing clearly spiritual work than when joining together to wash cars and share Christ or other examples.

For a brief period, I helped as a substitute teacher in local public schools. I enjoyed it because I love young people; I almost always subbed in middle and high schools. But one day, I decided to sub for a kindergarten class. Just once. My respect for kindergarten teachers went up about 1,000 percent that day! I was one-and-done for that. It was really a good day, just tiring. I know that great educators in kindergarten and elementary school find ways to make learning fun. There's no compromising in the learning process when we make it enjoyable. Why can't we do that as adults as well?

Mature believers should understand that they serve Christ not because it is fun, but because it is essential. God's ultimate priority is not to make us happy but to make us holy. But the Bible doesn't teach that being godly means being a sourpuss!

In Psalm 126, which describes the restoration of Jews to their homeland, we read: "Our mouths were filled with laughter, our tongues with joyful song" (Psalm 126:2). We have received a greater restoration in Jesus! Proverbs reminds us that "a cheerful heart is good medicine" (Proverbs 17:22a).

Evangelism causes such fear in so many people that the idea of having a good time while going out witnessing may sound too good to be true. But it is true, and it releases believers from many fears. If you've ever been on a mission trip or in some setting where a group teams together to do something 100-percent focused on God's work, you know the joy that brings. I have never seen a group of Christians more filled with a combination of laughter and joy with satisfaction and accomplishment than after hours engaged in servant evangelism.

I think we can agree that the quota for believers marked by laughter and joy has not been met. Too many are marked by fear: fear over politics, over the future, over so many things. Others are marked by anger. We need a joy infusion.

6. Servant Evangelism Gives Creative and Entrepreneurial Believers a Place to Shine.

This is a bonus; you don't need innovative or creative people. You can just put the examples you find here into practice. But why wouldn't we want to serve our creative God with the creativity and abilities He granted us? And what better place to do this than in tandem with the gospel?

Did you know that one in four Gen Zers hopes to make a living as an internet influencer? So many people are finding ways to become influencers on social media. (Some good, some not so much—being social-media savvy doesn't make you an expert.)

Shouldn't the church recognize and encourage people gifted by God to put those gifts to work for the gospel?

It can be something really simple, like the two men in a North Carolina church who bought cleaning materials and then went to local businesses offering to clean their restrooms or the wife of a new mission pastor in Indiana who gave away small packages of coffee as a means of both getting acquainted with the community and inviting neighbors to an evangelistic coffeehouse they started. This congregation also attended their citywide parade, giving away packages of candy with small cards containing information concerning the mission's activities. The pastor of the new mission later reported that these activities led to a number of baptisms.

I've met so many people in churches who love Jesus and want to serve Him. They show up week after week, singing on the praise team, serving in preschool, leading a small group, and doing so many other important things. Yet they wonder, "Is this all there is? What else can I do for my Savior?" Unleashing these people and giving them permission to find creative ways to share Christ may be a critical way to help them grow.

I once taught a class with a colleague for a semester where I wanted to encourage students to use their creativity. Our tradition was not known for its innovation, but I knew students who had abilities that weren't being used for the gospel. I personally invited some of them to take the class. The students each had to come up with a creative project to share Christ. The results were far more amazing than I expected:

- One student who performed hip-hop wrote a new song emphasizing the great Story of the gospel. I took him with me to a couple of places to do the song for youth groups.

- A student who majored in art at a major university brought four paintings, each with the same tree. Each was unique as the pictures displayed creation, the fall, the rescue through Jesus, and restoration. It was amazing!
- An athlete put together a presentation that illustrated the gospel through our physical bodies.
- A videographer created a fascinating video overviewing the gospel.

There were many others. That one class of about a dozen people showed the amazing creativity in the church.

Too many people in churches love Jesus and want to serve Him, showing up for services while wondering, "Is this all there is? What else can I do for my Savior?" Unleashing believers to find creative ways to share Christ may be a critical way to help them grow.

In their helpful book *Sent*, Ashley and Heather Holleman prayed for some time about how they might share Jesus and show kindness with their neighbors through hospitality. With elementary-aged children at the time, they needed to find a way to do so within the busy schedules they and their neighbors all shared. Their plan: they started preparing a big pot of soup every other Monday night, calling it "Soup and Stories." It was low-key: neighbors could pop in, have soup, and scoot if needed. The first night the Holleman's shared their story, including how they were often lonely and disconnected. They understood that hospitality calls for vulnerability, so they were honest about their own struggles rather than acting like they had it all together. That first night, a neighbor suggested that everyone tell a "breakdown, breakthrough, or breakup" story from their day.[1] She went first, breaking down in tears. This continued and led to other ways to connect with neighbors. They ended each meal with prayer, and over time saw several neighbors come to Christ.

7. Servant Evangelism Changes Not Only How the Community Views Your Church but Also the Way Your Church Views Evangelism.

I wish I had a dollar for every excuse I've heard for not sharing Jesus. I've had a few of my own. But this final point recognizes the power of servant evangelism to shift the perspective of those outside the church and in its fellowship.

There are people who are unchurched or dechurched whose thoughts about the church are anything but positive. Maybe they caricature all churches based on a bad experience they had at one time. Perhaps they see the church as full of judgment and lacking in grace. Maybe they obsess about the hypocrisy they've seen. Whether real or exaggerated, many aren't in our churches because of one or more reasons like these.

It's sad but true: there are many churches who could vanish from their communities tomorrow, and no one would notice. But when we are out in the community showing kindness, serving others, and being the hands and feet of Jesus, it makes an impact on the community.

Some churches have their people wear matching T-shirts with their church name. At our home church, Church of the Highlands, wear bright red shirts with SERVE TEAM in large white letters as we serve. We are easy to spot! This is a great way to develop a reputation for being the people who care for their communities. This is a good thing!

Churches will be revitalized when the gospel becomes prioritized. The good news is that more and more believers and church leaders see this and are beginning to respond.

For Review

1. Which of these seven reasons did you find most helpful or compelling? Why?

2. Were you surprised by any of these?

3. How can reflecting on these encourage you as you plan to be engaged in servant evangelism?

> Churches will be revitalized when the gospel becomes prioritized.

4
Commission
Sharing Jesus Effectively Today

When he saw the crowds, he had compassion on them, because they were harassed and helpless, like sheep without a shepherd. Then he said to his disciples, "The harvest is plentiful but the workers are few. Ask the Lord of the harvest, therefore, to send out workers into his harvest field."

—Matthew 9:36–38 NIV

Kindness . . . is what separates the good from the great.

—Bear Grylls

One of the reasons sharing Jesus is such a struggle for so many today is that we woke up and the world had changed. We see it everywhere, so I don't need to go into detail here except to say that today we see shifts in everything from marriage to identity, not to mention the rise of cancel culture. We are literally witnessing a global existential crisis about the meaning of life. What an opportunity!

In response to this:

We show kindness, and we share Jesus.

We speak the truth but do so in love.

We boldly declare good news with empathy and compassion.

We look to the early church who faced persecution, was misunderstood, had no political or economic power, and yet changed the world by sharing and showing Jesus everywhere they went.

It's time to recover that. But just how do we speak up about Jesus and tell the good news?

Establish a Baseline

Just as a physical exam helps to establish a baseline for your physical health to see what areas you need to work on to get healthier, I want to do a simple exercise to help you do the same as a witness. I've used this for years and have had many tell me how it has helped them get started without discouraging them.

But first a couple of statements you need to hear:

If you are God's child, He is not mad at you. He loves you. He proved that on the cross (Romans 5:8). If you never share your faith one time, your Father loves you. Yet, as His child, you want to worship Him and bear fruit for Him, right? You don't do this to earn His favor; you allow the Spirit to push you and grow you in your witness to show your gratitude to God and glorify Him (Matthew 5:16).

You are called to grow. You begin your Christian life as a spiritual baby and continue to grow as a disciple until He calls you home (2 Peter 3:18). It's in your DNA as a believer to grow, to take next steps. I want to help you grow as a witness because you were made for this.

Now the exercise:

Give your honest assessment that describes your current ability and activity as a witness who speaks to others about Jesus. Here is the scale from 1 to 3:

1. I can explain to someone else the good news of Jesus Christ, and I share my faith regularly as I have opportunity. I still get nervous but am excited to tell others about my Savior.

2. I can explain the gospel, though I'm not confident. I have shared my faith before but want to be more consistent. I miss opportunities and can learn more, but I do love Jesus and want to be more confident and consistent.

3. I've never shared Christ much (or ever) and don't know if I can. The thought of it terrifies me!

Again, these are not to discourage you but to help you establish a baseline. And it's OK to say you are a 1.5, a 2.5, or 3.5 (or four, five—you get the idea). What number would you choose?

Now, think about the next step you might take to help you move closer to a 1, or to learn even more if you are at 1. It's not where you are; it's where you are headed in your witness that matters most.

Wherever you are, if you know Jesus, you can start talking about Him today. And please remember these vital and practical points:

- Sharing Jesus isn't about giving a presentation but about having a conversation.

- You aren't a salesperson pitching a product; you are a new person in Christ with a story to share.

- You are part of the work of the Spirit, so you simply do your part. You don't save anyone! Don't pressure yourself to "close the deal." (Remember, we aren't salespeople.) Simply help people see and hear more of the good news about Jesus.

- As you talk to people, remember that you aren't trying to make a decision or a contact. You are trying to make a friend, then to introduce your friend to Jesus!

In this chapter, I want to offer four simple ideas to help your witness and lead others in theirs.

It's not where you are; it's where you are headed in your witness that matters most.

1. If You Have a Tool, Keep Using It

We all need a tool, a rubric, some simple way to communicate the amazing, good news. There are so many out there. I've used and taught everything from Continuous Witness Training (CWT), to Evangelism Explosion (EE), to The Story (www.viewthestory.com), and the Three Circles (https://www.namb.net/evangelism/3circles/), to name just some. The best tool for sharing Jesus is the one you are actually using! So, if your church already has a tool, keep using that. Even better, finding the tool you are most comfortable with is most likely to be the tool you will use.

2. Foundational Training

The gospel is amazing: it's so simple that a child can understand it, but after a PhD and decades of studying the gospel, I am still learning more about it. The Bible often summarizes the good news briefly as Jesus does in Luke 24:44–47:

> Then he told them, "This is what I told you would happen while I was still with you, that everything written about me in the law of Moses, the Prophets, and the Psalms must be fulfilled." Then he opened their minds so they could understand the Scriptures, telling them, "This is what is written: The Messiah was to suffer and rise from the dead on the third day, and that forgiveness of sins for all who repent is to be proclaimed in his name to all

nations, beginning from Jerusalem. You are witnesses of these things."

At Life Bible Study and Iron Stream Media, we produce an amazing resource that gives a simple and yet profound training built on the Roman Road approach. It's through the ministry Time to Revive (timetorevive.com). Their approach is very much in line with sharing and showing Jesus:

> LOVE: Love comes from God. Go out of your way. Go be amongst the crowd. Change your environment.
>
> LISTEN: Ask questions. Listen for the heart issue. Don't defend or argue.
>
> DISCERN: Discernment is from the Holy Spirit. Discern the Holy Spirit's leading. What's the point of entry?
>
> RESPOND: When we love, listen and discern, we are prepared to respond. The Holy Spirit does the work. When we respond God is glorified.[1]

They begin a conversation with kindness, asking, "How can I pray for you?" Time to Revive has multiple tools to help: a colored wristband, a card with key verses, and a marked New Testament, highlighting key words with these verses:

- Sin: Romans 3:23
- Death: Romans 6:23
- Love: Romans 5:8
- Faith: Ephesians 2:8–9
- Life: Romans 10:9–10

This is a proven, powerful, and simple way to learn to share Jesus. You need to learn the gospel message and how to share it with others.

If in the little exercise above you considered yourself a 3, this is for you. And it could help those who are a 2 while being a refresher for the 1s. Knowing what to say goes a long way in helping you to talk about Jesus.

3. Telling Your Story Is Powerful Today

Whether you consider yourself a 1, 2, or 3, there is power in simply telling your story about how Jesus changed your life. The Bible consists primarily of stories of people and peoples. We see testimonies throughout the Gospels (the woman at the well, man born blind, etc.); Paul shares his testimony in Acts 22 and Acts 26. The greatest defense of the gospel outside of God's Word is the story of a changed life.

You can start a conversation with almost anyone almost anywhere by simply asking them to tell you some of their story: "What's your story?" Once they've done that, they won't at all mind letting you tell yours. (That's called the law of reciprocity.) When you tell your story, if you know Jesus, you know you want to tell the story with Jesus as the hero and how He changes lives as the key point.

You can tell your story to anyone and everyone, at any time or place, sharing it in a way that, just as the story of David and Goliath points to a greater Story of God who redeems His people, your story points directly to God's bigger Story.

A helpful way to do that is to frame your story along the same lines as the biblical Story of the gospel (more on this below). This way it follows a plotline of creation, fall, redemption, and restoration like this:

Life before Jesus (relates to creation)

Realizing I need Jesus (fall)

How I heard the good news about Jesus (redemption)

How Jesus is changing me (restoration)

If you've never done so or haven't in a while, take some time to write out your story. Here are some questions to help. Answer the ones that apply.

Life before Jesus: What was your religious background? What things were most important to you when you were younger? What influenced you spiritually? What did you think about God then?

Realizing I needed Jesus: What caused you to see that something wasn't right in your life? What patterns or practices were you doing that you knew were wrong? What relationships, habits, thoughts, or actions made you question your beliefs? What were your thoughts about God at this time?

How I met Jesus: Who told you the gospel? What factors helped you begin to see its truth? Who were the people, books, songs, events, or other influences that helped you know Jesus?

How Jesus is changing me: How and when did you believe, surrendering your life to Him? How is your experience with God different now? The Bible? The church? In what ways can you see God working in your life now? How does a perspective of heaven and eternity impact you? How can you see God using you now?

Sharing personal stories is natural and helpful. You aren't marketing a God product; you are simply telling what happened to you. People are interested in these stories!

When you share this with someone, you can ask, "Has anything like that ever happened to you?"

4. Helping Believers to Share and Unbelievers to Hear: The Story of Life from Brokenness to Beauty

As I write this, I'm sixty-four years old—a young sixty-four! I can still remember a world where the church and the Christian faith were more prevalent and accepted in our American society than today. It resembled first-century Jerusalem in many ways. As the early church shared Christ with Jews—their primary audience at first—they did so with a common belief in the Hebrew Bible, that is, the Old Testament. A bit later as Paul began his missionary journeys, his custom was to start at the synagogue and speak to his own people, the Jews (Acts 13:14; 14:1; 17:2). When the gospel was shared with Jews, the focus began with the Old Testament teachings because Jews revered the Scriptures. Peter did so at Pentecost (Acts 2); Stephen did the same (Acts 7). When Philip encountered the Ethiopian eunuch (Acts 8), he did the same because the man was reading from Isaiah. When we talk with people who know the Scriptures (like the Jews) or have some level of respect for God's Word (like the eunuch), we can simply explain the Bible's core message to them.

But when Paul came to Athens, speaking to philosophers and others who didn't know or believe the Old Testament, what did he do? He spoke about a Creator who made our world; He also made us for a purpose, giving us a hunger to worship (Acts 17:22–28). He then explained how we need Him but can't find Him on our own (Acts 17:27–30). He called them to turn from sin and believe in Jesus, who through His resurrection brings life and hope (Acts 17:31; see verse 18). Some did believe (Acts 17:34). Before he preached to them, however, he was in the marketplace conversing with them (Acts 17:17).

People don't like being preached at or marketed to, but everyone enjoys a conversation. Did you know the average person has twenty-seven conversations a day? Introverts may have half that many, but we all are experts at conversations.

I want you to see a way to have a conversation with someone that connects the Story of God's great redemption and love with their story just as it connected with yours. Sharing Jesus this way in the context of showing kindness and serving others creates a much better pathway for spreading the good news.

The Biblical Story

I'm going to tell you a Story. It's a Story you will recognize because it's a Story we can see in other stories—from fairy tales to epics, from novels to movies. This Story is not mainly about you; you aren't the center of the Story. And yet, this Story is the way to make sense of your story. It's a Story you can talk about with others to show them the beauty and the wonder of the Story of Scripture that centers on Jesus and His work for us.

Behind every person's understanding of the world is a story that explains how they got to where they are. Whether we think about it consciously or not, but we are all living out a story that we are trying—or at least hoping—will make sense. Everyone lives out of the reality they know. That's a *worldview*, how we view the world. Our lives are truly a collection of many stories. The word that is bigger than mayonnaise for that is *metanarrative*. Every great novel has an overarching metanarrative: think of *The Lord of the Rings* for instance. Movies we love tell one big story but have a lot of smaller stories underneath, developing characters, foreshadowing the future, and more. Stories have plotlines that take us from one place to another.

Of all the stories of all time that try to tell us why we are here and what we are to do—not to mention what happens when we die—the Story of Scripture is the one that is true!

Steve Jobs famously observed that "the most powerful person in the world is the storyteller."[2] Almost a century ago, C. S. Lewis and J. R. R. Tolkien had conversations about stories and myths. These conversations helped Lewis—who was an agnostic—become a follower of Jesus. Tolkien explained to his friend and colleague that underneath all the stories and myths, we have a greater story. That story is the Story of God's redemptive work in Jesus Christ. All the other stories—from "Snow White" to a Hallmark movie, from Homer's *Iliad* to the Marvel Cinematic Universe—stir us because they touch on the greater Story, however incompletely. "The myths woven by us, though they contain error, reflect a splintered fragment of the true light, the eternal truth that is with God,"[3] Tolkien observed.

We are familiar with many common plotlines of stories from "man falls in a hole" (versions include "overcoming the monster" or "killing the dragon, rescuing the damsel"), "boy meets girl" (think rom-com), or "rags to riches" (*Cinderella*, for example). Here's my point and the point Tolkien made that helped Lewis see the reality of the Christian faith: the Story of redemption across the Bible is the greatest Story ever told and the only one that is completely true.

When you understand this, you can share Christ as a storyteller rather than selling Christ like a marketer. What parent hasn't read or told stories to their children? Who hasn't recounted the story of a movie or book we loved? Who hasn't given an account of a vacation, embarrassing incident, or exciting news to others?

I've found that telling people the great Story of the gospel and how it relates to their story has been the most effective approach I've ever used. It applies to someone who never heard the gospel and someone who thinks they know the Bible when all they ever really got was a religious take on the Scriptures. I've seen extremely far-from-God people come to faith and understand the Bible more as baby believers than some church attenders do who see the Bible only as a rule book.

I've written in chapter 1 about how in a world like ours, where growing numbers of people are nones and dones, it's vital to show God's love as we share the good news. But how we tell the Story is vital as well. I want to help you learn to share Christ in a way that is less intimidating to you and more interesting to those with whom we share. Even if they don't believe it when we share Jesus, we want them to wish what we are sharing were true.

What if I told you the gospel Story helps you—yes, you—to have conversations about everyday things we care about in such a way that we can show people how the desire for beauty and the disgust with brokenness is part of the gospel Story, and that of all the stories in the world, the gospel Story is the ONE that shows us how to get from broken to beauty? Let me give you an overview of this great gospel Story.

What I'm about to give you represents how I've shared the gospel for years now. At Life Bible Study we are excited to offer a new booklet to help believers have gospel conversations focused on this Story. The booklet can be left with people we encounter in our daily lives or at outreach projects. We call it *Life's Story . . . Brokenness to Beauty.* You can order copies at lifebiblestudy.com.

Every person you meet, including the person you see in the mirror daily, lives somewhere on a continuum between beauty and brokenness. If things are going well, life is beautiful, right? I literally have a sticker on my Mac that says "Life Is Beautiful" because I've seen God turn brokenness into beauty in my own life. But most people focus on what's broken. Our car broke down. We didn't get the raise, or someone disappointed us.

When I meet someone in a setting where we can have a conversation, like in a coffee shop, I love to ask (as I mentioned above with the testimony), "What's your story?"

Everyone likes to talk about themselves. And everyone has a story. You can learn a lot about someone based on how they answer this and describe themselves. We all have a story of our life that is made up of a collection of stories, each telling a story about one aspect of life. We have a story about our family, another about our musical or sports interests, yet another about our personality and idiosyncrasies, and so much more.

Here's an important assumption I make when talking with people about their story and God's Story. I assume people have some of God's Story right, and some of it wrong. I don't start with the idea that I have it 100 percent right while they are 100 percent wrong because that's just not true. It's also pretty arrogant. I assume they have it right somewhat but more wrong than right. In humility, I'm confident I have it mostly right, but I'm not 100 percent right because I'm still learning and I'm certainly still growing; I've not always faithfully lived out this Story. So, instead of starting from as far away from the person as possible on the spiritual side and viewing them as distant, I start as near to them as I can, figuring out what parts of the Story they get, then helping with the rest.

What could this possibly have to do with sharing Jesus and showing kindness? More than you might think. The conversation follows the main ideas of the larger metanarrative of Scripture: creation, fall, redemption, and restoration, using phrases like these:

We have a BEAUTIFUL WORLD.
We are BROKEN by sin.
We are still BELOVED by God.
We must BELIEVE to be restored to God.

Here's the question I ask to get into this Story from God's Word: "Isn't it a **beautiful** world?"

I've posed this question to servers at a local restaurant, college students in Greece, Buddhist monks in Thailand, and a self-described free thinker in Paris. Everyone, without exception, agrees with me that it's a beautiful world. Because *it is a beautiful world*. Ask them what they love most about our world. You can talk about animals and plants, the beach, and the mountains. Some people can talk for hours about their pets. Point out how when we are stressed and want to get away, we go to nature to see the ocean or walk through a forest. Hunters and fishers will talk about their favorite spot; some will describe their museum of choice. The possibilities are endless.

There are two main ideas from Scripture I'm noting through this conversation. *First, God made a beautiful world.* We see this in Genesis 1, John 1, Romans 1:20, and throughout the Bible.

Second, God made us uniquely different from anything else. This is obvious. I'm referring to the image of God or *imago Dei*. I'm not trying to convince someone from Scripture at this point; I'm just having a conversation about what we can see: that our world is different, and we stand out in this world. We were created in the very image of God (Genesis 1:26–28). I will ask, "Have you noticed how people are different than anything else?"

You can talk about how we are different rationally. We create things: we developed the internet and traveled to the moon. Beavers build a dam, but we provide electricity to a whole city with one. Birds can fly, and so can I because of airplanes. We ask questions like "Why?"

In the course of the conversation, you can add how we are differently spiritually. People want to be part of something bigger than themselves. We are drawn to wonder; this can be seen in how we make art. We admire beauty. St. Augustine captured this beautifully in his prayer: "You have made us, oh God, and our hearts are restless until they find rest in you."

After talking about this you can ask:

"But something has gone wrong in this world, hasn't it?" Again, I've asked this countless times across America and in over a dozen countries on four continents, and I'm still waiting to meet someone who disagrees with that. Often a person will start naming examples. I might say, "Our world is marked by **brokenness**."

Sin entered the world, and things have been cracked and broken ever since. Theologians call this the fall. Two themes emerge. First, this *brokenness brought with it separation and death.* This means separation from God and from one another (Romans 3:23; 6:23). We see division and outrage all around us. We experience disease and ultimately death. You can talk about these things as you converse. You can also be vulnerable and real rather than sounding holier-than-thou by talking about issues in your own life where brokenness has been painful.

Second, while we are all aware of this brokenness in our world and our lives, *we try to fix it ourselves.* That's what Adam and Eve did when they sinned: they hid in shame and guilt, trying to cover themselves with fig leaves. People still do that today. I will often point out how no parent ever had to teach their child to disobey. That normally elicits a chuckle from the person I'm talking with because it's so obvious.

We try so many ways to fix our brokenness:

- Some try to numb the pain, developing addictions to substances.
- Some try to fix it with a relationship, hoping the next one will make things right.
- Some pursue self-esteem through power, position, or possessions.

- Some try to be religious or hope to do more good deeds than bad.
- Some create their own ideology in defiance of God.

Here's the unvarnished truth: *we can't fix ourselves.* We are like Shakespeare's Lady MacBeth washing her hands, trying but failing to remove her guilt. We try but can't fix our broken lives.

Can you see how this conversation focuses on obvious things we see in our world and our lives, things that bring out both beauty and brokenness? This brings us to the place in the conversation where good news matters, and good news is available through Jesus.

At this point you can say, "There is good news: we are still **beloved by God.**"

Romans 5:8 is one of the most beautiful verses in all the Bible. God proved or demonstrated that He loves us. How? Jesus Christ, God's Son, died for our sin. Jesus came to this earth, born of a virgin. He lived a sinless life. He died a brutal death for us. He became the substitute for us before a holy God because of the love of God. Paul unpacks this in detail in Romans, arguing that God is righteous, we are not, and something must be done about our sin. That something is Someone named Jesus (Romans 3:21–25). Jesus legally took our guilt and shame on Himself, so that when we trust Jesus as Savior, we stand before God as someone declared not guilty. We who are guilty became not guilty because Jesus took our penalty. Jesus did more: He turned the criminal courtroom into an adoption hearing where the Father makes us His children. Paul talks about our broken creation and our broken lives being made new (Romans 8:20–23).

You can say, "This is why Jesus came and died for us: not to make us straighten up but to give us a new life. He didn't come to make bad people become good but to make spiritually dead people come alive!"

I like to talk about grace—God giving us what we don't deserve and mercy—God withholding judgment we do deserve. This is our great God who loves us and calls us to be His children (Ephesians 2:4–9).

Here is where we move to call the person we're talking with to a response. How do we respond to what God has done through Jesus to turn brokenness into beauty? How can God literally begin to rewrite our story with His Story?

You can say, "When we **believe Jesus is Lord and Savior**, we will see our brokenness turn to beauty."

We confess (which means to agree with God) that Jesus is Lord, turning from sin to a Savior (called repentance in the Bible), and believe God raised Him from the dead (Romans 10:9–10). God's cure for our brokenness is described beautifully in the New Testament: we experience a new birth. We are saved or delivered. We've been justified from guilt, reconciled with God, redeemed from sin's bondage, and more. When Paul calls it the gift of God in Ephesians 2:8–9, he isn't kidding. It's the greatest gift! Our sin earned spiritual death (Romans 6:23); we receive salvation as a gift by believing.

Turning brokenness into beauty means restoration. We all know what it means to restore an old piece of furniture or a musical instrument. It becomes new. God makes us new through Christ, restoring us to His purpose for our lives. We love movies with some version of "happily ever after" because we yearn for restoration ourselves. When we stop trying to write the story ourselves and let God write His Story through us by the power of His Spirit, we begin experiencing restoration with God. Ultimately, we will enjoy that in its fullness when God makes all things new in the new heaven and earth (Revelation 21).

As Christians, we believe that the Story of Scripture centered on the good news in Jesus is the Story that best tells the way the world really is—with its beauty and its brokenness, its joys and its sorrows, and its purpose and pain. That means it's normal for us to talk about Jesus as being the rescuer we all seek, the only One who can turn our brokenness into beauty.

Here is where you can talk about how God created each of us for a purpose: to know and serve Him. The good news (gospel) means we don't get to joy by seeking our way but by turning to God to restore us from brokenness to beauty and giving us a purpose. He made us with the personality and abilities we have; now we can use those for something far bigger than us. And we continue to learn and grow in this journey until Jesus returns and God restores all creation from broken to beautiful for all eternity!

God gives us His Spirit to guide us and the church to help us grow. Our response is to turn to God by faith.

You can lead the person you're talking with to pray a simple declaration of consecration to Jesus, turning from sin and surrendering to Him. If you are blessed to be able to do that, you will want to encourage them toward GROWTH:

> **G**—Go to God in prayer daily. I like to tell new believers (1) talk to God about everything; (2) your prayers are as valuable to God as any "great" Christian.
>
> **R**—Read God's Word daily.
>
> **O**—Obey God's Word.
>
> **W**—Worship weekly in a local church.

T—Tell others about Jesus.

H—Honor God's call for water baptism.

This is the amazing, true Story we get to tell others. We get to live this Story ourselves. What a great God we serve!

For Review

1. Which of these four approaches did you find most helpful or compelling? Why?

2. Which of these might be most effective in the community where your church is found?

3. Have you thought about sharing the gospel more as giving someone a presentation or having a conversation with them about the good news?

As Christians, we believe that the Story of Scripture centered on the good news in Jesus is the Story that best tells the way the world really is—with its beauty and its brokenness, its joys and its sorrows, and its purpose and pain. That means it's normal for us to talk about Jesus as being the rescuer we all seek, the only One who can turn our brokenness into beauty.

5

Implementation

Organizing the Whole Church to Live on Mission

That in the coming ages he might show the incomparable riches of his grace, expressed in his kindness to us in Christ Jesus.

—Ephesians 2:7 NIV

If his grace in kindness is "immeasurable," then our failures can never outstrip his grace.

—Dane Ortlund

"I want this."

Jessica said these words in response to hearing the gospel following our meal. She was our server at a Mexican restaurant on the edge of Baltimore on a late Sunday evening. As she said those words, I looked over at the busboy, whose name we learned was Timmy. He'd been eavesdropping on our conversation; both he and Jessica trusted Jesus that night.

Our group having dinner in an empty restaurant helped two young adults follow Jesus by faith. That doesn't happen every day, but why did it happen on this day? It started with showing kindness. When Jessica greeted us, we all gave her our attention and spoke kindly to her. We treated her like a person. As she took our orders, I said (as I typically do), "Jessica, we are going to say a prayer before we eat. Is there anything we can pray about for you?" She had never been asked that before, so she had to think about it. But after a few minutes, she happily asked us to pray for her schoolwork.

At the end of the meal, we left a generous tip, but before that Jessica said, "You are the nicest people I've waited on in a long time." I replied, "Well, the truth is it's late for me, and I can get grumpy. But Jesus changed my life, and we love telling others about Him." I opened a little gospel booklet and—wanting to be careful not to take too much time while she was on the clock—was about to give it to her when she did something unusual: she pulled up a chair and sat down with us. "This place is empty, and I want to hear more," she said. Soon Timmy walked up as well, and both received Christ.

The goal of this book, the projects suggested, and the witness training included is to create a mindset in believers to show kindness daily and share Christ with those we meet.

> The gospel has not lost its power, we've just lost our focus.

Let's say this is something new to you or something you haven't done lately or as part of an ongoing strategy. How do you get started? What do you need? Here are a few essentials.

1. Look Up to God

Don't start with a project or place; start with prayer. The early church in Acts started in a prayer meeting, not a think tank (see Acts 1). It doesn't matter how great our method may be or how excited we are; gospel work must start by saturating our plans with prayer and serving in the power of God's Spirit. Gospel work is spiritual work. We are at war with the Evil One for the hearts of people. Gather leaders and seek God's face. That's a given for anything a church does, but it matters so much more when we do work that assaults the kingdom of darkness.

> As you pray:
>
> - Pray for momentum as you begin talking about servant evangelism.
> - Pray for those who will be participating as well as those who will be reached.
> - Pray for a growing love for Jesus, a burden for souls, and for the brokenness and division in our world to push disciples to take action through showing and sharing the good news.
> - Pray Christians would be influenced less by social media and cable news and more by the Word of God.
> - Ask God for souls, for lives to be changed, for impact. Pray for wisdom and great faith.

I mentioned Psalm 126 earlier, which has a beautiful Old Testament connection to New Testament evangelism. The people are rejoicing because they have been released from captivity to be restored to their homeland. They've been physically redeemed. The Psalm ends with a compelling call to reach others:

Those who sow in tears will reap with shouts of joy.

Surely one who goes out weeping and carrying seed
to sow

Will certainly return with shouts of joy. (Psalm 126:5–6)

Have you "sowed in tears" for the lost lately? I'm not asking this to make you feel bad but to make a point: it's easy in the church today to go through life and never have our hearts broken over the lost.

Years ago, I did something often in churches that gave a public invitation—as nearly all the churches I spoke at did—when I spoke about sharing Christ. Before the service, I had stacks of gospel booklets across the front. At the invitation, I would ask the congregation first to think of someone they knew who didn't know Jesus and to pray for them. Second, I asked them to consider—I did not guilt-trip them—to do something specific. If they would agree that week to give one of the gospel booklets to the person they prayed for, I asked them during the invitation to come and take that booklet as a public commitment. In almost every case, the vast majority responded, and pastors shared testimonies with me later.

I should mention that I would always say to the people taking the booklets that if they didn't know what to say when they gave it to the person, just say "We had this preacher at our church this week who encouraged us to give this booklet about Jesus to someone, so I'm just doing what he asked us to do." Just that simple. True story: a young man told me he did just that, and, for the first time in his life, he led someone to Jesus—the guy he gave that booklet to!

I mention this to illustrate how more people in our churches want to honor the Lord and tell others about Him, but they need some encouragement and simple advice about how to do so. James Clear is right when he says: "Many people think they lack motivation when what they really lack is clarity."[1]

2. Look Around to Your Community

As you think about the community where God places your church, you can think of serving in two ways: the deep, long-term needs and the simple, everyday ways to serve. The former might identify the needs for ongoing ministries like a food pantry, tutoring/mentoring at local schools, or more. These are crucial but are not our focus here. Don't underestimate the impact of simple acts of kindness in Jesus's name over time on your community. One church I know began offering "Free Pizza Friday" once a quarter after the great recession of 2008. The church couldn't afford to pay for people's light bill or their mortgage, but they could offer a meal. The impact of that simple act over time was so powerful. I knew a young lady who was part of that church who started working at a place where all of her coworkers were nonbelievers. Most were pretty cynical toward the church in general, but the first time she spoke to one about the Lord, she mentioned her church. "Oh, that's the free pizza church, right?" her coworker replied. "I've never been there, but that's really cool what you do." Free pizza Friday opened many opportunities for her witness.

In most communities, efforts like a free car wash or helping people pay for laundry in laundromats are effective. I confess the car wash is my favorite. And going door-to-door, even when giving away useful items to people, is not as accepted or effective in many areas today. But it may be just fine where you live, so knowing your community is vital.

If you are new to the area or looking for fresh ideas, you can get some ideas by talking with people in key positions. And you can put servant evangelism into practice while you do so! One place to go is to first responders, the fire station, and the police station. But when you go, take a plate of fresh-baked cookies or something else to them! They may have ideas about ways to show Jesus's love, and they may help you find locations for car washes and more.

Another place that's helpful in many communities is a local restaurant. If you are in a smaller town, servers in restaurants are often very helpful. But you will want to start by showing these servers Jesus's love as well. In the next chapter, I will spell out how. And the local schools can provide insight and opportunities.

3. Look Inside the Church with a Next Steps Mindset

Every pastor and church leader wants to help disciples of Jesus grow. The way to do this is to develop a *next steps* mentality. Every believer can take next steps in their spiritual growth. Pastors can take next steps as well. Paul believed this: "I do not consider myself to have taken hold of it. But this one thing I *do*: Forgetting what is behind and stretching out toward what is ahead, I press on toward the goal—the prize of the heavenward calling of God in Christ Jesus" (Philippians 3:13–14). That's a next steps mentality!

In your church, you have people at a variety of stages in their growth. Some are babies spiritually, while others are leaders; and you have people all in between. That's true whether we are talking about volunteering, giving, praying, or witnessing. We want them—wherever they are—to be taking next steps in growth over time. That's the mindset you want to have as you encourage people to move from never witnessing, to being open to it, to participating in outreach, then to becoming a consistent witness.

Looking inside your church community with a next steps mindset helps in two specific ways. First, it helps with organizing outreach projects as you find people to serve. Second, it identifies needs that must be filled and training that will help people take next steps. If you have very few people who can share their faith, you may want to do some personal evangelism training first. In fact, whenever possible you should include basic witness training as part of your preparation. That way, as servant evangelism becomes more a part of your church, the witness training you provide will help to equip and encourage people to move from the support teams to the outreach teams described below. And you want to remind everyone regularly that this is all practice for showing and sharing Christ at work, in the neighborhood, at school, and so on.

How would planning servant evangelism projects best be implemented through your current organizational structure? If Sunday school classes are primary, consider organizing through them. If small groups in the home is your strategy, organize through them. Or you can organize by age groups, especially in a smaller church (a youth project, college, young adults, etc.).

Identify people who can witness to be on each team. Who are people already able to lead a team, be the point person on sharing Jesus, or lead in setting up? The following pages will detail how to do this in a way that involves everyone and moves people to take next steps. You may unearth some leaders you weren't aware of in the process.

You probably have people who can help in this in many ways: a businessman who can donate items to be used in service to others, an owner or manager of a store in a great location for a car wash, and many more.

Tell believers how they can all be a part of this. The church is strengthened when everyone sees a way to participate. We want everyone to feel a part of the team, and there are no benchwarmers on God's team! I've sometimes seen pastors shame those who don't immediately join in efforts like this. Most of the time this is unintentional—we've seen that modeled; we are frustrated because it seems people don't care, or we feel as leaders that we aren't leading well if everyone doesn't immediately jump on board. I've also seen very intensive kinds of evangelism training unintentionally create a division in the church between the "real soul winners" who are trained and everyone else who isn't.

That's not the culture we want to create. There are two critical ways to help create a healthier culture. First, by fostering the attitude that everyone can contribute to reaching people—which we all believe is vital—evangelism can be a remarkable resource for unity when we have a "you are all a part" mentality rather than praising only those who are bold in their witness. Second, this prioritizes a perspective that is more "join the movement/be part of something bigger/you were made for this" than "if you don't get involved, you just don't love Jesus." The latter doesn't work, but the former approach is powerful!

Instead, think in terms of concentric circles where everyone in any circle plays a vital role. Ask those who can't physically participate to do the **praying**, those not ready go out to help by **supporting**, the timid to do the **serving**, and the bold to do the **sharing**. After my back surgery, praying was my one option for a season, and I was fine with that. Your goal over time is to see as many as possible move from the outer circle to the inner circle. And remember, senior adults can be a part of going to restaurants, wrapping presents at Christmas, and more!

The Whole Church Engaged in Showing and Sharing Jesus

As you can see, everyone in these circles is part of something bigger. Instead of berating those who won't go out or ignoring those who can't, call on them to be on the support team. As you do these outreach events, remind people that they can take next steps to the next circle. And when someone comes to Christ, remind everyone they played a part!

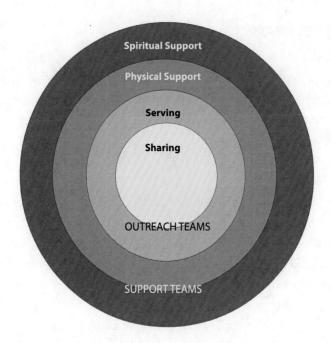

This organizes people into two main teams, each with two groups.

Support Team

These are all the people who won't or can't be out doing the projects. They are vital! There are two groups here: spiritual and physical support.

Spiritual Support

People who can't go to do the projects can pray. The same holds true for those who make excuses for not participating. Show them a way to be involved and watch many of the "I won't" excuses go to "I want to" as they are encouraged to be part at a level where they are comfortable.

Physical Support

This would primarily be those who don't feel ready to go out as part of the projects. Their role is huge: they can provide childcare for parents, set up the area where the teams assemble, ensure that materials are ready, provide refreshments/prepare a meal when appropriate, and so much more.

Outreach Team

These are the people involved out in the community (or interacting directly with people in a church-based event) showing and sharing Jesus to those outside the church. NOTE: You will probably have people who can overlap the serve and share teams. Some who are ready and willing to share their faith can take a turn serving, and vice versa. People can be involved across these circles. While one person may do the witnessing, everyone takes part in the experience. The person pumping gas or washing a windshield prays in tandem with the prayer team as another witnesses. The same is true for those on the support team who prepare gift packages or baked goods to be delivered door-to-door to evangelism prospects.

Serving

These are mostly people who are afraid to share verbally but are happy to participate otherwise; those to whom we say, "I promise you don't have to say anything!" They may be people who want to share Christ but want to watch someone do so first. They wash the cars, give out the flowers/light bulbs/water/everything else. Why would we want to complain about these people simply because they don't feel equipped or confident to share Jesus? If you plan a year of servant evangelism projects every month, these are the very people who the first month refuse to talk but within a few months can't stop talking about Jesus!

Sharing

These are the people who are willing and able to speak to people about Jesus. Over time you will want to offer training in sharing Jesus verbally to increase the numbers here. Here's one thing I know: there are many people in your church who would share Jesus openly and confidently if they knew a basic way to share Jesus and saw it practiced a few times. I've seen this countless times, and there are few things more exciting to a leader than to have a believer who never witnessed become a passionate evangelist!

For Review

1. What are ways you believe God is calling your church to be a part of showing kindness and sharing Jesus?

2. How is your church's organizational structure set up for outreach opportunities?

3. Everything in this resource is aimed at helping you and your church in ways that fit how He has led you to this point. How might you apply or adapt the circles above with the four groups to your vision and mission?

Every pastor and church leader wants to help disciples of Jesus grow. The way to do this is to develop a *next steps* mentality. Every believer can take next steps in their spiritual growth.

6

Vision

Ideas for Sharing Jesus and Showing Kindness

I led [Israel] with cords of human kindness,
with ties of love.
To them I was like one who lifts
a little child to the cheek,
and I bent down to feed them.

—Hosea 11:4 NIV

You can accomplish by kindness what you cannot by force.

—Publius Syrus

Several years ago, I was feeling pretty good about the writing I was doing and the books I'd written. Too good, in fact. At the time—perhaps prompted by the Spirit to take me down a notch—I picked up a John Steinbeck novel. After reading Steinbeck, I decided I should probably never write anything again! Reading a master like that can give perspective. Here is something Steinbeck observed about writers: "A man's writing is himself. A kind man writes kindly. A mean man writes meanly. . . . A wise man writes wisely."[1] I think you can apply that to a church. A church can have a vision focused on standing for truth—a good thing. But that can easily lead to a culture that doesn't interact well with those who aren't believers, though Jesus did so without sin (Luke 5:27–32). A church can have a vision of love that ignores unchanging truth, leading to acts of service without the bold declaration of the gospel. But a church with a vision for disciple making, that like Jesus is full of grace and truth (John 1:14, 17), will stand firmly on the gospel and show kindness to those in need of its life-giving power. We can't have a vision for only one or the other. Truth without grace is mean; grace without truth is meaningless.

A vision for sharing Jesus and showing kindness works in any church setting: big cities and rural communities, in the American heartland and a Ukrainian village, from Paris to Peoria. It's the simplest way to adapt to a given cultural context. It can be done door-to-door or hut-to-hut, in an urban park in Eastern Europe, and in a megachurch in the American South.

Remember this as you serve others: this is not a bait and switch. You serve no matter how they respond, and you never give any expectation that they should do something for you because you served them, just show kindness in Jesus's name.

The following ideas are only examples. You can dream of more. (And you should!) The following are offered to help get you started but also to stimulate ideation with your church.

1. The Big Five

In strength training, we have the big five: dead lift, squat, bench press, overhead press, and pull-up (or the pull-down machine). If you do these with correct form and consistency, you will get stronger.

Here are my big five categories for showing and sharing Jesus with one or more examples of each. They may not all fit your specific context, but offering these with a little more detail on how to do them might stir more ideas for where you are.

1. Public Spaces

These are projects you do with a group out in public in your community. Get as much permission as you need (setting up in a park may require a permit, for instance). My favorite is the **free car wash**.

What you need: A place (a business is better than the church facility usually, but not near a car wash business!); washing equipment (hoses, nozzles, buckets, soap, brushes, rags, towels); signs that say in big letters "FREE CAR WASH" and "NO DONATIONS"; for witnessing, you need chairs, a cooler filled with ice and water bottles (and sodas if you like) for the people whose cars you are washing, a canopy for shade if needed, gospel booklets, a few Bibles or New Testaments, and a card or something with brief info on your church. Plan for about four hours as experience shows that unless you've advertised it ahead of time, it will take some time to generate cars to be washed. Also, make sure you have sunscreen and you've told everyone involved to dress appropriately (no bikini car washers!).

What to do: Pray together before you begin. Designate who will do what, though people will need to switch from washing, to holding signs, to helping with witnessing. Be sure someone capable of sharing Christ is always at the seated area. Tell the group that under no circumstances will you receive donations. This is our gift to the community and, like salvation, will cost the recipient nothing because someone else paid for it!

Set up the car wash area and the place where people will sit with several chairs, the cooler, and materials. As cars begin to show up, encourage the people to get out and enjoy the shade and free water while their car is washed. Make sure they park their car; we do not drive their vehicles! Some may prefer staying in their car, and that is fine. We serve them no matter what, and we do a good job. At the end of their wash, you can still offer them literature. But most people will get out and are open to talk because they are surprised the car wash is free.

What you will find is that many people will insist on giving a donation; some will be adamant. Don't take anything when they offer. I normally reply with, "Thanks for the offer, but this is our gift to you and our community. And it's a reminder that Jesus offers us salvation as a gift!" The reason people want to do this is because of the law of reciprocity, which says that when a good deed is done to one person they want to reciprocate. You can smile and say, "You are welcome to join us at our services this Sunday!"

One more thing: as you wash the car, pay attention to conversations going on. If someone is really listening while the gospel is being shared, you don't want to walk over and say, "Your car is finished!" Just keep washing slowly.

A second example is the **laundromat.** With discernment and grace, you can show and share Christ in certain public places where people have time on their hands. This could be a bus stop or in a park, for instance.

What you need: First, a lot of quarters—the first time I did this, one older lady brought a month's worth of laundry! It cost me over twenty-five dollars (and that was years ago), but she trusted Jesus, so it was worth it! Both males and females should be involved in this as it is a bit concerning for a lady alone at a laundromat to be approached by a couple of men. You will also need connect cards and gospel booklets. At one laundromat, we had no clearly positive response while there, but the next day someone visited the church services because a card was left there. They were too shy to talk, but the card connected with them.

What to do: As you see someone sitting and waiting on their laundry, have two of you (male and female, preferably) say, "Hi, we're from _____ church, and we would love to pay for your laundry, if you don't mind." Be very sensitive to give space to them, and if they aren't interested, don't press. What you might see happen is after a few minutes, they will come to you and ask if you are serious. (They don't see this every day!) You can also ask if you can pray for them about anything. At one church in South Carolina, I had three students (one guy, two ladies) and a dad of one of the ladies join in. We did these visits for three straight days and saw a number of people come to Jesus, and some believers were really encouraged.

2. Routine Places

This exemplifies the "add without subtracting" mindset, where you simply add showing kindness in everyday contexts, sometimes together as a group. I've seen a number of people become followers of Jesus with **servers in local restaurants.** Here's how to do this as a small group or ministry together:

What you need: a group of believers who go to the same restaurant (or if a large group, multiple restaurants), divided into groups of about 3 to 5 each to be seated across the restaurant. Bring with you: a number of ink pens with a rubber band around them for each group; a dozen or two donuts to give to the hostess to put in the break room for the workers to share; some connect cards and gospel booklets; and the ability to tip well—it doesn't have to be outrageously large, but it certainly shouldn't be under 20 percent of the bill. Oh, and bring an appetite!

What to do: Let the hostess and the servers know you are out as a group from your church just enjoying fellowship together and encouraging the community. Give the donuts to be placed in the break room. You can write, "We love you, (church name)" and add some church connect cards. Ask the server's name and thank them for serving you. When they take your order, have someone in the group ask the server for any prayer requests. Pray for these as you say grace. Later as they come by, give them the ink pens (I've had servers almost come to tears, thankful for this simple act of kindness). Leave a generous tip. If the server seems interested, you can ask him or her to meet up sometime when they are off work for coffee with several of you. More than once, I've seen someone come to Christ when we met for coffee like this. People are often more interested in talking about spiritual things than we are!

I've read notes from restaurant managers who thanked groups of believers who've done this. The managers didn't seem to mind that the groups also shared Christ briefly and respectfully; they just loved seeing their employees loved on!

> NOTE: When witnessing in a public place remember the wisdom of R. A. Torrey: (1) Obey the Holy Spirit, and (2) Don't embarrass the person.

3. Local Community Events

Often you can just tag team with something already happening in your community that provides help without being a nuisance. For instance, you don't want to give away cases of free water at the baseball park if selling drinks is a big way for them to raise funds. An example I've seen is a **booth at the local town festival.**

What you need: permission required to host a booth, and a well-prepared booth with people to serve.

What to do: A great booth is simply a prayer booth (instead of the old kissing booth!). People can drop by, give prayer requests, and receive prayer. There's no reason *not* to share Christ then! Have resources about your church and people there who are comfortable praying on the spot with those who come by.

4. Your Church Facility

My favorite examples here are these two: **free pizza Friday** and a **community block party.**

I've seen churches plan and host a big block party on their property with great success. Collecting clothes and other needed items beforehand can help. Providing free hot dogs and drinks or other food items, setting up games, bounce houses, and more can allow your church to serve people from your community.

What you need: With free pizza Friday, you can speak to area pizza restaurants as some will gladly offer a discount for a large number of pizzas. Spread the word a couple of weeks prior and perhaps give free tickets for church members to pass out. It may be hard to guess the number of people who might come at first, but once you begin doing this, you will have an idea of your area. You may also speak to a local ice cream store about individual ice cream sandwiches to hand out. You'll need volunteers to set up and tear down tables and chairs, serve the food, and clean up.

What to do: You will want to have people who can share Christ floating around just getting to know people and talking with them. I've observed that what churches don't do is get up and preach the gospel to the crowd. You might mention your service times as you welcome people or introduce a couple of leaders throughout the night, but don't give any hint of a bait and switch. Serve them food and talk to the people who are open. (I know from personal experience many will be!) And then thank everyone who came. I've invited unchurched friends to come to these, and they did. One fellow remarked to me how surprised he was that there wasn't a time-share presentation (his term for preaching the gospel to him). I told him no, we weren't doing that, but I appreciated him letting me talk to him about Jesus.

5. *Your Everyday World*

It bears repeating again: the aims of these organized efforts at showing and sharing Jesus are to help believers learn to think like servants and share their witness in everyday life. Reflect on the people you interact with all the time, the places you go, and the influence you have. How can you begin small steps of service and kindness to open ways to share Jesus? Here are a few ideas, some noted previously:

- Getting to know servers in local restaurants, praying for them as you dine.
- Helping a neighbor work on a car or paint and clean their garage.
- Going to a neighbor's child's ball game.

OK, this is really simple, right? That's the point. I'm talking about a mindset shift that thinks more about impacting people for Christ by our deeds and our words in small ways over time. This is the vision: increasing numbers of believers showing kindness and sharing Jesus, growing in confidence, and finding ways to care for others, until a disciple-making movement erupts!

2. Other Great Ideas

The following are adapted from Steve Sjogren (https://www.ste-vesjogren.com/94-servant-evangelism-ideas-for-your-church/).

1. Giveaways at Public Places

You may not have many opportunities to share the gospel as people are heading to their cars in these instances, but you can still bring a brief moment of joy and say, "We're from _____ church and are just sharing the love of Jesus in a practical way!"

- Bottled water giveaway: Attach a card with your church's name, website, and service times. You just need a place, a cooler full of water, connection cards, and smiling faces.

- Soda giveaway: Same idea but have diet or regular sodas. Adding water in this setting is harder as more choices in a brief time span complicate things. Just ask, "Regular or diet?"

- Coffee/hot chocolate giveaway: For cooler weather but the same idea: two containers with regular and decaf coffee or a third with hot chocolate. You will likely want to have a small table for cups and lids, creamer, and sugar/sweetener options.

2. Door-to-Door Giveaways

If your community has places where door-to-door is effective, try some of these:

- Light bulbs: A four-pack of 60-watt bulbs works great. Put a contact card from your church and/or a gospel booklet with each pack. Just tell people to be careful as they carry them. Tell them everyone needs light bulbs at some point, and Jesus is the light of the world!

- Popcorn: Give packs of microwave popcorn with a contact card from your church attached. Tell people as they pop it to think about popping into your church. (I know, it's corny!)

- Flowers: Carnations are especially affordable. Go door-to-door (like the first day of spring, for instance) and give a carnation to each home.

- Leaf-raking, mowing services: Look for lawns with high grass or lots of leaves. With a crew of several mowers or rakes, you can knock out a yard in no time while someone speaks with the homeowner.

- Fruit giveaway: People love fruit! A banana, apple, and orange in a clear plastic bag with a connection card is perfect.

3. Serving Local Businesses

Serving local businesses is a way to bring good will and open gospel opportunities. Ask businesspeople in your church about ideas in addition to these:

- Restroom cleaning: This is Steve Sjogren's favorite. Put together a portable cleaning kit (with heavy duty gloves!) and watch store owners' and managers' amazement when you offer to clean their restrooms for free. Don't be surprised if they refuse because it's not something they see every day!

- Business blasts: Show up at businesses with simple gifts with cards from your church. You could tie this to a specific day (like a dozen donuts on National Donut Day, the first Friday in June). Note: these are only for employees, so they don't think you are soliciting their customers.

4. Specialized Services

These may require a bit more expertise and planning but are fantastic ways to show Jesus's love.

- Single moms' oil change: This one is for single moms only but is both for moms in your church and in the community. For those already in your church, have them sign up with their make and model ahead of time so you can have their oil filter ready. This needs to be at the church and should only be done by experienced people. If you can't sign up community single moms ahead of time with their car info, you might have a runner ready to go to a nearby auto parts store.

- Christmas gift wrapping: Providing free wrapping is popular before Christmas. Some stores will let you do this inside. (I've seen local Walmarts do this.) You will need to have the paper, tape, and people ready ahead of time for this. In some smaller communities, you may be able to spread the word that you are doing this service at your church at certain hours and days.

- Door-to-door Scotch Tape: Speaking of wrapping gifts, who hasn't run out of tape while wrapping? Giving out tape with a connect card—yes, taped to it—is a great, inexpensive idea.

- College campus service projects: If your church is near a college, you can find a variety of ways to connect with students. See if you can have teams help students on move-in day. Have a late-night pancake dinner at the church during exams. Put together care packages for freshmen. (Some studies say college freshmen are the loneliest people.)

3. Choose to B.L.E.S.S.

We can also learn from other churches who discover a way to share Jesus and show kindness. Dave Ferguson, cofounder of Community Christian Church in Chicagoland and head of EXPONENTIAL, uses a concept called B.L.E.S.S. It's simple, practical, and something that could help move believers into a lifestyle in their neighborhood and other areas of influence through a simple process. Here's a brief overview:[2]

B—Begin with Prayer

A daily time of prayer is the perfect time to ask God how He might want to expand our life to include others.

L—Listen

Can you imagine the ground we could gain for the kingdom if we would just get better at listening. Just think about the change we would see in our world if instead of vocalizing our differences on Facebook or Twitter, we would just listen—listen to people's hopes and dreams, their struggles, and their fears. God, help us to bless others as we listen to them.

E—Eat

Sharing a meal and asking Jesus to be there is the secret sauce for experiencing community. Jesus ate meals with people all the time. Eating with someone is like putting salt on food. You're giving that relationship flavor. You're helping it to taste even better.

S—Serve

As you pray, listen, eat, and build relationships with those around you, it will become apparent how you can serve them.

If you listen carefully enough, people will tell you how you can BLESS them.

S—Story

When the time is right, and I think it will be apparent, share you story of how you found your way back to God. Talk about your struggles, the challenges you've faced, the doubts you've had along the way.

You can find a list of more ideas in the Appendix.

For Review

1. Based on these ideas, what are others that could be effective where you live?

2. Begin making a master list of options in your area based on the categories listed above.
   - Public spaces
   - Routine places
   - Local events
   - Church events
   - Everyday life

3. Go to the Appendix or to https://www.stevesjogren. com/94-servant-evangelism-ideas-for-your-church/ to see whether any other ideas there might be useful.

> A vision for sharing Jesus and showing kindness works in any church setting: big cities and rural communities, in the American heartland and a Ukrainian village, from Paris to Peoria.

7

Prioritization

Calendaring Your Impact

*Do you disregard the riches of his kindness, forbearance,
and patience, unaware that God's kindness is meant
to lead you to repentance?*

—Romans 2:4

Be kind first, be right later.

—James Clear

I love pastors, church leaders, and churches. I've spent most of my life training church leaders and serving in thousands of churches as a speaker or teacher. In each case, my first goal is to bring glory to God. But closely following that is this goal: I want to serve and assist the person who invited me. I'm not called to that church, they are. So, I want you to know my heart as to why I wrote this resource. I didn't write it to convince you to do this or to do it just like I've written. I wrote it to be an aid, whether you find one quote or the whole book helpful. If you are leading your church well to show and share Jesus, you don't need more information. If I only encourage you to keep doing what you're doing, that's a win! Or, if you can simply take ideas here or there that you've read and put them into ministries that are already rolling, I thank God for that.

Turn a Moment into a Mindset That Becomes a Movement

Throughout this book, I've intentionally sought to encourage and inspire while giving helpful ways to show and share Jesus. But I must give you an honest caution in two specific areas from years of past experiences. First, I've seen a youth group implement this at a DNow or a church host a big serve day. It goes well; people involved are animated and excited, and we often hear stories of salvation, learn of needs in the community, and find people interested in the church. There is talk about how this has great potential for the mission of the church. But that's as far as it goes. The success of the day doesn't translate into momentum moving forward. I think a reason for this is that so many churches are event driven rather than guided by system or process. But when this becomes a part of the ongoing system of the church and its disciple making, the moment of outreach becomes a mindset within the church, leading to a movement of revitalization in disciple making.

This is one reason I'm a big fan of the D-Life approach of Bill Wilks. It builds into the small group methodology and outreach emphasis every other month. Find out more about D-Life at www.livingthedlife.com or check out the resources at www.lifebiblestudy.com.

I'm not against one-time events, but why have a flash in the pan for a moment (spiritually speaking) when you can have a steady fire for evangelism stoked by consistent servant evangelism outreach that creates a mindset of serving and sharing? This doesn't have to take over your church, but it can be a vital part of how you "do" church in every ministry. And it's easily added to a lot of things you are already doing.

The second area I've seen churches get sidetracked is by getting excited about serving people but sharing Jesus gets left out. I get it; evangelism made most believers freak out before the pandemic and the dramatic cultural shifts over the past few years. But these shifts call us to renew sharing Jesus with a passion, not to set it aside while serving people who need the life-giving message of the gospel.

Getting Started

If you want to help a believer, church, or organization to see what they are most passionate about, ask them to evaluate their bank account and calendar. It's not a stretch to say that how we spend our money and how we spend our time shows what we care about most.

The good news is that servant evangelism is the best value in ministry: you can do better with less cost than almost anything else. Talk about a spiritual bang for the buck! And though it can be integrated into activities and emphases already at work, it will require intentionality to become part of the calendar. We are generally so busy that adding something else can be overwhelming.

Think about change in three buckets:

Bucket one is what doesn't change. There are fixed costs and vital calendar issues for people, families, churches, and organizations.

Bucket two is what is no longer effective. For most of us, we waste some time and money regularly. What could be cut in time and spending that would make space for gospel advance?

Bucket three is what can be adapted. Add a block party at the end of vacation Bible school. Turn Saturday afternoon of a DNow event into an outreach activity. Add time to your daily walk in the neighborhood to speak to neighbors you meet and ask them for prayer. Adding without subtracting can help your integration of your witness with your life.

If you're new at this, here are a few practical ways to get started:

1. Pick a Date for an Inaugural Servant Evangelism Day.

Ideally, this should be a Saturday in warm weather free of any other events on the church calendar. These schedules are all adaptable. They simply reflect the way I do the training.

Tentative Big Serve Saturday Schedule

- 8:30–9:00   Light refreshments and fellowship
- 9:00–10:30   Training
- 10:30–11:00   Break and role-play sharing Christ
- 11:00–12:00   Training
- 12:00–1:00   Lunch and organizing the teams (Be sure someone is on each team who is comfortable sharing Christ.)
- 1:00–3:30 or 4:00   Servant evangelism projects
- Conclude with a thirty-minute share and celebration time.

NOTE: (1) After this initial training, you can go straight to projects on future Saturdays. Many churches do this from around eight to nine a.m. to about noon. (2) The training can be abbreviated to condense the day based on your schedule.

Tentative Sunday Schedule

- Worship service(s): preach a message focusing on showing and sharing the love of Jesus (John 4, Colossians 4:2–6, for example).

- Training time: if you have Sunday school classes at one hour and worship services during a separate hour, you can do the training overview of servant evangelism then; otherwise, you can do so during lunch.

- Organize teams.

- Send out the teams for two and a half hours or so.

- Follow with report time (see below).

Keys for a Successful Servant Evangelism Day

Here are ways to prepare for a big servant evangelism day:

Three Months to a Year Prior to the Day

1. Determine what projects you will do: Have some that can be done indoors in case of rain. Plan the schedule accordingly. Car washes need three hours or more usually, but that's too long for going to a restaurant to serve servers, go door-to-door, or some other projects. Send out the longer project teams first. You can add projects to the list as people sign up and bring ideas. It's better to do fewer projects well than to overextend. Budget accordingly based on the projects. Everyone will need connect cards and some way to capture information from people.

Three Months Prior to the Day of the Event

2. Enlist the people: Sign up people to participate based on the four categories and two teams (support and outreach) in the last chapter. Note: You as leader will want to sign up first and encourage other key leaders

to sign up for the outreach team. You will always have people ready to help with the support team, so be more intentional with enlisting people for outreach. You want to encourage as many as possible to be part of the projects going out. You can use ideas, stories, and other content from this book as you promote.

3. Get supplies ready: church connect cards (If you don't have these, you can simply print business cards with the church name, website, physical address, and service times.); gospel booklets; some New Testaments/ Bibles; some format to collect information on people who make decisions for Christ, who share a need, who are interested in the church, etc.; materials for the specific projects. If you have teams going door-to-door, print maps with their street clearly marked and be sure not to send two teams up the same street!

Some churches set aside a closet or other space to keep supplies for these projects ready.

Within One Week of the Event

4. Train the people: I've found it far better to do everything in one day on the first day, with the exception possibly to give personal witness training (chapter 4) earlier. Using this book as a resource, one of these two options works well:

> A. Saturday: Take the morning to overview what servant evangelism is, why it's important,

and clearly lay out the plan for the day. Don't overwhelm with information; just share the key ideas.

B. Sunday: Depending on your church's schedule, and as noted above, you can give an overview of servant evangelism in the Sunday school hour, and then in the service, use the message time to preach on sharing Jesus and showing kindness. If your church has small groups during the week or has multiple service and Sunday school times on Sundays, you can have leaders lead the eight-week, small group study of this book.

Note: for small groups that meet in homes, challenge them to use one week a quarter or every other month to do servant evangelism as a group during group time!

5. Send them out: be sure the church staff are all on teams!

6. Report time: Gather the people for report time after. This is a huge enthusiasm builder. I like to use a marker board and put a list of things (whatever you list you will want to tell the teams before they go out), including totals for people connected with, testimonies/ gospel shared, booklets/connect cards given out, any prospects for future outreach discovered, any specific needs, and (I like to have fun with it.) a place to tally strange or humorous incidents, biggest surprise from the day, etc.

> **Within Two Weeks Following the Event**
>
> 7. Evaluate and plan the next one: This day is not a one and done but the starting point. Get together with key leaders and plan the next day.

2. Build Momentum over Time

Servant evangelism done one day, one time can be a great moment for your church; servant evangelism as an ongoing ministry can help to initiate a movement of caring and sharing.

Once you've started to implement evangelistic service projects into your church, continually remind people that these projects, as vital as they are, are simply practice for every day of life. What you want to see is more than a good number of people involved in projects (though that's awesome); you want to hear stories of couples who prayed for their server, a family who served a neighbor in need, and a coworker who served a fellow employee in Jesus's name. This is a powerful way to help believers see ways to live missionally in their daily lives.

ANNUAL: Big Serve Day or Serve Week Each Year in the Summer

In July 2023, over twenty-five hundred churches joined together for an annual serve day alongside the Church of the Highlands in Alabama. Churches from Atlanta to Los Angeles, Colorado to Canada had people wearing matching shirts and smiles, showing and sharing Jesus. There are also churches who set aside an entire week each summer for a local mission trip to their own community. Events like this take more planning and can include projects that require greater expertise like the single moms' oil change, building a wheelchair ramp, painting school classrooms, or more. You could possibly do all the big five above that would apply to your community.

If you only did this each year, it would make a major impact for Christ. But what if this were only part of a larger process? Here are more examples:

Quarterly or Bimonthly

I would argue that having a day monthly to give attention to servant evangelism is ideal, but if that's a bit overwhelming, think about having these once a quarter or every other month.

If your church uses D-Life, the groups are already encouraged to participate in an evangelism project every other month.

You can schedule these days at a set time, like the first Saturday of each quarter, or you can time them to events like some or all of these:

Valentine's Day
First day of spring
Easter weekend
Mother's Day
Father's Day
Summer block party
Back to school bash
Fall festival
Christmas season

Monthly

Ideally, have a day a month for servant evangelism projects. This model applies the first Saturday of each month (except on a holiday).

Some can be repeated multiple times. (Larger churches could have three or four car washes for instance.) I've listed some examples, but you may have people who just like to do the same thing every month. The guys I mentioned who cleaned toilets did so monthly, and sometimes I joined them! Your climate makes a difference too; I've lived in Indianapolis and Houston, so you can guess which one needs snow shovels in the winter.

It's much easier to simply have a set Saturday each month. I love how we have the big serve day in July and then a monthly serve day at Church of the Highlands, along with other ongoing service opportunities. Serving others is in the DNA of the church. It's much easier for people to remember and set up their calendars when the date is consistent and then take note of the exceptions. Here are examples using 2024 as the year:

ONE—First Saturday Monthly

January 6

February 3

March 2

April 6

May 4

June 1

July 6 becomes July 13: This would be the annual Big Serve Day and moves from a potential conflict near the July 4 holiday.

August 3

September 7

October 5

November 2

December 7

TWO—Monthly Calendar Tied to Key Dates with Outreach Ideas

January 6: laundromat coin giveaway, business toilet cleaning, restaurant ministry

February 3: popcorn for Super Bowl (on February 11), Valentine donuts for fire/police stations, restaurants (Valentine-shaped donuts for the break room are a hit!), or businesses

March 2: 9-volt batteries for smoke alarms, bottled water giveaway, free car wash, Easter activities (Easter is March 31, so have Easter invite cards printed and available by March 1.)

April 6: free car wash, bottled water giveaway, light bulb giveaway, restaurant ministry

May 4: Mother's Day carnations (Mother's Day is May 12.), small American flags for Memorial Day, lawn mowing, trash pickup

June 1: End-of-school block party

July 6 or 13 (based on holiday impact of July 4): annual serve day/week

August 3: free car wash, school supplies for needy families

September 7: back-to-school bash

October 5: batteries for smoke alarms, light bulb giveaway, restaurant ministry

November 2: serve local businesses and schools

December 7: have Christmas invite cards printed by here, toy drive for needy families, free Christmas wrapping

For Review

1. How does your church budget and calendar reflect showing kindness to others (the Great Commandment) and sharing Jesus (the Great Commission)?

2. Which of these calendars might be the best starting place for you?

> Servant evangelism can turn a moment of ministry into a mindset among God's people, leading to a movement of disciple making.

CONCLUSION

Evangelism Is Caught More Than Taught

Have you ever been reading through the Bible when suddenly you saw something so obvious you couldn't believe you'd missed it until that moment? It might be a verse you've read that suddenly revealed an insight you hadn't seen. You may have gone through a season that caused certain themes to show up, making some verses stand out like never before.

I had one of these aha moments while riding along I-85 with Jeremy, a young man who volunteered to drive me to a number of speaking engagements while he was a student. Jeremy was a unique fellow; he was a beast of an athlete, and he had a shaved head except for the unshaved shape of a cross on the back of his head. And, he had a unique combination of passions: studying the Hebrew language and sharing Jesus.

As we cruised down the interstate, I was reading the early chapters of Acts. I'd read Acts many times and took a course on the book in seminary. But as I planned to speak that night from Acts 4, I saw a word repeated in the early chapters I'd never noticed before.

The word? *Daily*. It shows up by my count over ten times in Acts, and it's also implied repeatedly as we see the church continuously on mission. Some examples are:

- "*Every day* they steadfastly continued in one accord" (Acts 2:46).
- "And *every day* the Lord added to their number" (Acts 2:47).
- The lame man was "put *every day* to beg" when he met Peter and John (Acts 3:2).
- "And *every day* . . . they never stopped teaching and proclaiming the good news" (Acts 5:42).
- Some widows were neglected in the *daily* food distribution (Acts 6:1).
- Churches grew *daily* (Acts 16:5).
- Paul was "in the marketplace *every day*" and was "preaching the good news about Jesus" (Acts 17:17–18).
- Paul witnessed *daily* in Ephesus (Acts 19:9).

In addition, many passages in Acts show the daily practice of faith with examples of continuous witness and acts of kindness (Acts 4:31–35; 6:7; 8:4–8; 9:22; 10:48; 11:19–21; 12:24; 13:4–5, 49; 14:7, 21–28; 16:5).

Would you like to move from being a Sunday-to-Sunday, church-attending kind of Christian to a daily, missional one?

Are you ready to move from a path-of-least-resistance, minimal commitment to a daily, passionate, lifestyle of living for Jesus?

Start thinking of your faith as a daily lifestyle rather than a Sunday event. Begin focusing each day on intentionally showing kindness while seeking to share Jesus. Join with other believers to do the same regularly.

I had a friend once I saw after a long time apart. I didn't recognize him; he'd lost eighty-five pounds! I asked him what happened. He said he went to his doctor for a checkup and was told he was now a diabetic. The doctor gave him an honest overview of what that meant. (Short answer: it's not good.) That was the shock my friend needed.

He started exercising at night. Nothing fancy; he just started moving and increased the intensity over time. Every. Single. Day. No exceptions. And in just over a year, he was down eighty-five pounds and had kept it off. He also changed his eating habits which made a massive difference.

We often think that the more we are in God's Word, the more we will live it out in our witness. The opposite is more generally the case. The more we step out in faith to make an impact for the gospel, the more we see how we need God's Word. It changes our spiritual diet, if you will. My friend changed his diet once he saw the impact of his exercise. The same might be true for you. Just start daily, intentionally showing and sharing Jesus and see what happens.

ONE-DAY MISSION TRIP

You can host Doc Alvin Reid or a certified trainer at your church or ministry for a one-day mission trip experience where you learn to show and share Jesus followed by going into the community together. For more information, send an email with One-Day Mission Trip in the subject line to alvin.reid@ironstreammedia.com.

APPENDIX

More Ideas[1]

Service Ideas	Ways to Implement	Materials Needed
Neighborhood windshield washing	Go door-to-door washing windshields in driveways.	Cards, squeegees, squirt bottles, cleaner, shop rags
Mother's Day carnation giveaway	Set up outside grocery store on Saturday before Mother's Day.	Cards, table, sign
Snow removal	Help people dig out.	Cards, shovels, coffee
Pulling out cars stuck in snow	Rescue people from ditches or otherwise stranded.	Cards, shovels, chains, bag of grit or salt pellets, coffee
Return empty garbage can from street	Bring cans back to people's houses.	Cards
Food delivery to shut-ins	Deliver food.	Cards
Car drying at self-serve car washes	Help dry cars after they have been washed.	Cards, towels, or a couple chamois
Outdoor window washing	Wash first-floor windows.	Cards, professional squeegees, cleaner, short ladder, buckets
Yard cleanup	Find messy yards.	Cards, bags, rakes

Easter basket giveaway	Every child wants an Easter basket.	Cards, baskets vary (candy, Christian literature) Once we put in Christian tapes.
Rainy day grocery escort	Help shoppers to cars with packages.	Cards, golf umbrellas
Instant camera pictures	Find people or couples at parks or malls and take pictures.	Cards, cameras (Stickers for back of photos are best.)
Windshield washing at self-serve gas stations	Revive the practice of free windshield washing with fill-up.	Cards, squeegees, squirt bottles, red rags, cleaner
House/apartment repair	Fix broken things. Limit repairs to your capabilities.	Cards, basic tool kit
House/apartment/ dorm cleaning	Who doesn't need their place cleaned?	Cards, vacuum cleaners, brooms, trash bags
Winter car wash	Spray salt and road grime off undersides of cars	Cards, coffee, wands
Summer car wash	Free car wash! Use banners that say, "Free Car Wash—No Kidding."	Cards, basic washing equipment, banners. You can also serve drinks and play music.
Filling windshield washer fluid	Refill washer reserves in cars and clean wiper blades.	Cards, washer fluid, signs, table
Scraping out fireplaces	Remove ashes with small flat shovels.	Cards, small brooms, shovels, possible initial investment on tools

Checking air in tires	See if tires are properly inflated. Adjust pressure if necessary.	Cards, compressor or portable air bubbles, air pressure gauges
Memorial service	Advertise complimentary memorial service in newspaper.	Cards, set up and take down
Radon detectors	Give out detectors in areas where radon is a concern. Return in a few days.	Cards, detectors
Carbon monoxide detectors	Give out carbon monoxide detectors.	Cards, detectors
Smoke detector batteries	Give out smoke detector batteries.	Cards, reminders with date, batteries
Toilet cleaning	Clean toilets of restaurants and stores.	Cards, urinal screens, cleaning supplies
Light bulb service offering to change burned-out bulbs	Go door-to-door with light bulbs, cards, stepladder.	Supply fifteen 60-watt bulbs
Laundromat outreach	Pay for washing machines and dryers at local Laundromats.	Cards, rolls of dimes or quarters
Blood pressure screening	Check people's blood pressure at public places.	Cards, stethoscopes, sphygmomanometers
Car safety light check	Replace burned-out bulbs in cars.	Cards, variety of spare bulbs to replace burnouts, screwdrivers
Killing weeds	Spray for weeds and poison ivy on sidewalks and driveways.	Cards, weed killer, sprayers, gloves, masks

Seal blacktop drive-ways	Help homeowners seal driveways. Use flyers to get interest.	Cards, sealer, sealer brooms
House gutter cleaning	Clean gutters on houses of leaves, sticks, and debris.	Cards, gloves, ladders, trash bags
Birthday party organizing	Organize and run parties for children. Advertise in local papers.	Cards, music for party
Door-to-door food collection for the poor	Distribute flyers door-to-door, then return a week later to pick up cans and dry goods.	Cards, bags given out
Car interior vacuuming	Set up in mall parking lot/gas stations to vacuum cars.	Cards, several canister vacuums, several hand-held vacuums
Leaf raking	Who likes to rake leaves? We do it for them.	Cards, rakes, bags Blowers work well but are more expensive.
Christmas gift wrapping	Everyone needs his or her gifts wrapped. Do it at the mall for free!	Cards, paper, tape, scissors, etc. Build a simple kiosk or booth.
Lawn care	Find unkempt lawns and go for it.	Cards, can do basic mowing or more
Soft drink giveaway	On a hot day, nothing refreshes like a cold drink in Jesus's name.	Cards, drinks, ice, clean plastic trash cans for storing cans on ice, table
Free coffee	Set up tables at store exits or sporting events.	Cards, table, two to three containers, creamers, sugar, stirrers, sign: "Free Coffee"

Popsicle giveaway	Set up tables at store exits or sporting events and serve Popsicles.	Cards, table, two to three coolers, ice, sign
Windshield washing centers	Hit every car in the lot at stores and shopping centers.	Squeegees, squirt bottles with window cleaner, red shop rags, cards
Grocery store bag packing	Go to a self-bagging grocery store and help people bag their groceries.	Cards, might wear matching aprons, buttons with "just because"
Pictionary in the Park	Start playing Pictionary and strangers show up.	Cards, white board and markers, Pictionary cards
Balloon giveaway	Go to a park and give balloons/ cards to children with parents.	Cards, helium tanks, balloons
Complimentary bird feeders/refills to convalescent hospitals	Share God's love with shut-ins.	Cards, bird feeders, birdseed
Free house number painting on curbs	Paint address numbers on the curb.	Cards, stencils, spray paint
Free community dinner	Throw a party for a neighborhood.	Cards, food choice: two to five dollars per person
Free coffee giveaway at a major bus stop	On cold days, hot coffee is nice.	Cards, coffee, cups, two large, insulated containers, condiments
Free instant pictures at horse carriage stands	Set up shop at a downtown horse-drawn carriage stand.	Cards, cameras, film

Shopping assistance for shut-ins	Shop for shut-ins.	Cards, vehicles
Collect trees after Christmas for proper disposal	Meet a practical clean-up need.	Cards
Doggie dirt cleanup of neighborhood yards	Clean up doggie messes.	Cards, pooper-scooper or use plastic bags over hands, bags
Shoe shining service	Shine shoes for free at stores, malls, and other public places.	Cards, shoe polish, rags Kits are great.
Feeding parking meters	Feed expired meters; leave a note.	Cards, lots of change

Resources to Help You Share Jesus and Show Kindness

1. Eight-Week Small-Group Study

- Designed for small groups of any size/age or large group study over eight weeks
- Includes going into the community on mission twice to show and share Jesus over the eight weeks

2. Three-Session, Youth Disciple Now Small-Group Study

- Friday night, Saturday a.m., and Saturday p.m./Sunday a.m. studies
- Designed to help send out students on mission on Saturday afternoon of a DNow event

3. Mission Trip Preparation

- Equip teams for showing and sharing Jesus in any cultural context
- Includes going on mission once or more in your community before the mission trip

Find these resources here:

Notes

Introduction

1. Steven Pressfield, *The War of Art: Winning the Inner Creative Battle* (New York: Rugged Land, LLC, 2002), Kindle Locations 68–69.

2. Ross Douthat, "Waking Up in 2030," *New York Times*, June 27, 2020, https://www.nytimes.com/2020/06/27/opinion/sunday/us-coronavirus-2030.html.

1. Momentum

1. Edward E. Moody Jr., "The Top Ten Challenges Facing Churches in 2023," *Great Commission Research Journal* 15, no. 1 (April 1, 2023): 19–25, https://place.asburyseminary.edu/cgi/viewcontent.cgi?article=1419&context=gcrj; David R. Dunaetz, "Growing and Declining Churches Face Different Challenges: A Statistical Analysis of the Top Ten Challenges Facing Churches Study," *Great Commission Research Journal* vol. 15, no. 1 (April 1, 2023): 27–42, https://place.asburyseminary.edu/cgi/viewcontent.cgi?article=1420&context=gcrj.

2. "The Greatest Need of Pastors: A Survey of American Protestant Pastors," Lifeway Research, https://research

.lifeway.com/wp-content/uploads/2022/01/The-Great est-Needs-of-Pastors-Phase-2-Quantitative-Report -Release-1.pdf.

3. Jim Davis and Michael S. Graham, *The Great Dechurching* (Grand Rapids: Zondervan Reflective, 2023), 3.

4. Gregory A. Smith, "About Three-in-Ten U.S. Adults Are Now Religiously Unaffiliated," Pew Research Center, December 14, 2021, https://www.pewresearch.org /religion/2021/12/14/about-three-in-ten-u-s-adults-are -now-religiously-unaffiliated/.

5. "Modeling the Future of Religion in America," Pew Research Center, September 13, 2022, https://www .pewresearch.org/religion/2022/09/13/how-u-s-reli gious-composition-has-changed-in-recent-decades/.

6. Daniel A. Cox, "Generation Z and the Future of Faith in America," Survey Center on American Life, March 24, 2022, https://www.americansurveycenter.org/research /generation-z-future-of-faith/.

7. Cox, "Generation Z and the Future."

8. Jeffrey M. Jones, "U.S. Church Membership Falls Below Majority for First Time," Gallup, March 19, 2021, https:// news.gallup.com/poll/341963/church-membership-falls -below-majority-first-time.aspx.

9. Alan Cooperman, "Religious 'Switching' Patterns Will Help Determine Christianity's Course in U.S.," Pew Research Center, September 29, 2022, https://www .pewresearch.org/short-reads/2022/09/29/religious -switching-patterns-will-help-determine-christianitys

-course-in-u-s/#:~:text=Over%20the%20last%2015%20 years,16%25%20to%20nearly%2030%25.

10. Alvin L. Reid, *Evangelism Handbook: Biblical, Spiritual, Intentional, Missional* (Nashville: B&H Academic, 2009), 77.

2. Passion

1. Jim Davis and Michael S. Graham, *The Great Dechurching* (Grand Rapids: Zondervan Reflective, 2023), 126.

2. Davis and Graham, *Great Dechurching*, 113. Emphasis added.

3. Alvin L. Reid, *Join the Movement: God Is Calling You to Change the World* (Grand Rapids: Kregel, 2007), 19.

4. "'The Only Thing We Have to Fear Is Fear Itself': FDR's First Inaugural Address," https://historymatters.gmu .edu/d/5057/.

3. Mobilization

1. Heather Holleman and Ashley Holleman, *Sent: Living a Life That Invites Others to Jesus* (Chicago: Moody, 2020), 132.

4. Commission

1. "Learn How," Time to Revive, https://www.timetorevive. com/training.

2. "Steve Jobs and Thomas Edison: The Power of a Story Well Told," Pythia, https://pythia.international/strategy #:~:text=Jobs%20asked%20a%20small%20group, generation%20that%20is%20to%20come.%E2%80%9D.

3. Humphrey Carpenter, *Tolkien: The Authorized Biography* (Boston: Houghton Mifflin, 1977), 147.

5. Implementation

1. James Clear, *Atomic Habits: An Easy & Proven Way to Build Good Habits & Break Bad Ones* (New York: Avery, 2018), 71.

6. Vision

1. John C. Maxwell, *The 16 Undeniable Laws of Communication: Apply Them and Make the Most of Your Message* (Duluth, GA: Maxwell Leadership, 2023), 19.

2. Dave Ferguson and Jon Ferguson, *B.L.E.S.S.: 5 Everyday Ways to Love Your Neighbor and Change the World* (Washington, DC: Salem Books, 2021), 25.

Appendix

1. Adapted from Alvin Reid and David Wheeler, *Servant Evangelism: Showing and Sharing Good News* (Wake Forest, NC: Gospel Advance Books, 2013), 48–55.

About the Author

Alvin Reid—or Doc as many know him—is Director of Life Bible Study, an imprint of Iron Stream Media, a Christian media company in Birmingham, Alabama. He loves helping pastors and other leaders make disciples who make disciples. He also works with leaders as a coach, speaker, teacher, and more through Doc Reid Coaching.

Over four decades, Alvin has spoken at thousands of events in churches, on scores of college campuses, and at conferences nationally and globally. For many years, he taught in Christian higher education with a focus on evangelism, discipleship, youth ministry, and spiritual awakenings. A prolific author with over twenty books written or edited, he is a certified coach and speaker with the John Maxwell Group.

Doc Reid has a BA from Samford University, and both an MDiv and a PhD from Southwestern Baptist Theological Seminary. He and his wife, Pam, live Gadsden, Alabama, where they enjoy spending time with their kids and grandkids most of all!

He continues to lead training in evangelism, leadership, and more in churches and youth ministries, as well as encouraging and equipping leaders.

If you want to invite Alvin to your church or ministry, please reach out at docreidcoaching.com or email him at alvin.reid@ironstreammedia.com.